Soup

THE AUSTRALIAN
Women's Weekly

contents

The scent of a simmering soup wafting from the kitchen is second to none on the appetite-whetting meter. Add to this the facts that soups are fairly easy to make and virtually limitless in range, and you'll be as fascinated with making them as we were when developing the recipes for this book. Delicious and healthy sustenance in a single saucepan, here is a selection of old favourites updated and even more exciting new concepts that will have you reaching for your stockpot.

Pamela Clark
Food Director

soup, beautiful soup

In a perfect world, every soup would be made with homemade stock. However, no matter how good our intentions, more often than not our time-poor lives find us having to resort to the packaged variety. Thankfully, today's manufactured product has come a long way since the era of the stock cube, with both tetra-packed and canned styles being more than adequate, especially when used in robust multi-ingredient soups with dominating flavours. Some of the recipes in this book do require the real deal, but just about all of them will be the better for it. See the recipes at the back of this book to discover how easy it is to make your own stock and how much more delicious your soup will taste when you do.

Soup, the world's best known "bowl food", is a whole meal in a single take; it may have been around almost since the discovery of fire but has never lost its appeal. Soup warms us in winter, cools us in summer, and fills us without making us feel uncomfortably full. And it can potentially supply us with our daily nutritional needs in one neat package. From a clear and delicate Asian broth to a hearty peasant stew, soups cover all the right bases – aroma, flavour, texture, substance. Depending on our mood, we can slow-cook a bean and shank soup, fill zucchini flowers for poaching in a fragrant consommé, or quickly toss a can of soup with a few fresh vegies and serve it with herbed toast. A perfect soup is a relaxed way to cook and an equally relaxed way to consume a whole meal.

Accompaniments can bring a soup to life. Some soups have a traditional accompaniment that's essential to the recipe, like gruyère croûtons on french onion soup or a salty cracker crumbled into chowder. Others need to be bulked up or enhanced by a contrasting texture and that's when wontons, noodles, dumplings and pasta come into the picture. Soup can be complemented by an abundance of possibilities, from a simple scatter of freshly chopped herbs to any number of different breads – from shop-baked sourdough and ciabatta to homemade damper or scones. Fresh cheese, crème fraîche or yogurt; pesto, pistou or salsa; sour cream or yogurt; rice patties, ravioli or spätzle: you name it, there's a perfect accompaniment for every soup. The final choice is ultimately up to you as the creative cook, but a little thought should go into the process because the accompaniment should harmonise with and complement the individual soup's heritage, purpose, content and flavour.

Seafood

asian prawn and noodle

3 cups (750ml) water
3 cups (750ml) fish stock
10cm stick fresh lemon grass (20g), chopped coarsely
4 fresh kaffir lime leaves, torn
8cm piece fresh ginger (40g), sliced thinly
2 fresh small red thai chillies, chopped coarsely
1 tablespoon fish sauce
1kg uncooked medium king prawns
100g rice stick noodles
230g can bamboo shoots, rinsed, drained
100g fresh shiitake mushrooms, sliced thickly
3 green onions, sliced thinly

1 Place the water and stock in large saucepan with lemon grass, lime leaf, ginger, chilli and sauce; bring to a boil. Reduce heat; simmer, uncovered, 10 minutes.

2 Meanwhile, shell and devein prawns.

3 Strain broth through muslin-lined sieve or colander into large heatproof bowl; discard solids. Return broth to same cleaned pan with noodles, bamboo and mushrooms. Simmer, uncovered, about 5 minutes or until noodles are just tender. Add prawns; simmer, uncovered, about 5 minutes or until prawns are cooked.

4 Serve bowls of soup sprinkled with onion.

• **preparation time** 10 minutes **cooking time** 20 minutes **serves** 4
per serving 1.3g total fat (0.3g saturated fat); 757kJ (181 cal); 9.6g carbohydrate; 30.4g protein; 2.3g fibre

Chowder is thought to have originated on the Atlantic seacoast of North America where fishermen at sea would cook a portion of each day's catch in a flour-thickened stew and eat it with any available bread on board, no matter how stale. Thankfully, the tradition has evolved, and today the standard accompaniment is a salty cracker or a water biscuit, crumbled by the handful into the individual bowl of chowder.

fish chowder

40g butter
1 large brown onion (200g), chopped coarsely
1 clove garlic, crushed
2 rindless bacon rashers (130g), chopped coarsely
2 tablespoons plain flour
2 medium potatoes (400g), chopped coarsely
3 cups (750ml) milk
2 cups (500ml) vegetable stock
400g firm white fish fillets, chopped coarsely
2 tablespoons finely chopped fresh chives

You can use any firm white fish fillets, such as perch, ling or blue-eye, for this recipe.

1 Melt butter in large saucepan; cook onion, garlic and bacon, stirring, until onion softens.
2 Add flour; cook, stirring, 1 minute. Add potato, milk and stock; bring to a boil. Reduce heat; simmer, covered, about 10 minutes or until potato is just tender.
3 Add fish; simmer, uncovered, about 4 minutes or until fish is cooked through (do not overcook). Serve bowls of soup sprinkled with chives.
• **preparation time** 15 minutes **cooking time** 30 minutes **serves** 4
per serving 19.5g total fat (11.6g saturated fat); 1810kJ (433 cal); 28.4g carbohydrate; 34.8g protein; 2.4g fibre

creamy scallop with caramelised leek

40g butter
4 shallots (100g), chopped finely
2 cloves garlic, crushed
3 cups (750ml) water
3 cups (750ml) fish stock
¼ cup (60ml) dry white wine
2 medium potatoes (400g), chopped coarsely
1 tablespoon plain flour
½ cup (125ml) cream
350g scallops, without roe
1 tablespoon finely chopped fresh chives
caramelised leek
20g butter
1 large leek (500g), sliced thinly
1 tablespoon white sugar
¼ cup (60ml) dry white wine

We suggest you make your own stock for this recipe; see the recipe on page 113.

1   Melt half the butter in large saucepan; cook shallot and garlic, stirring, until softened. Add the water, stock, wine and potato; bring to a boil. Reduce heat; simmer, uncovered, about 15 minutes or until potato is just tender. Remove from heat, cool 15 minutes.

2   Meanwhile, make caramelised leek.

3   Using back of teaspoon, work remaining butter into flour in small bowl.

4   Blend or process soup, in batches, until smooth. Return soup to same cleaned pan; add flour mixture. Return to a boil, stirring, then remove from heat. Stir in cream and scallops; stand, covered, 3 minutes.

5   Serve bowls of soup sprinkled with leek then chives.

caramelised leek Melt butter in medium saucepan; cook leek, stirring, about 5 minutes or until softened. Add sugar and wine; cook, stirring, about 15 minutes or until leek is caramelised.

•   **preparation time** 20 minutes (plus cooling time) **cooking time** 40 minutes **serves** 4 **per serving** 27.3g total fat (17.4g saturated fat); 1827kJ (437 cal); 24.2g carbohydrate; 17.3g protein; 4.1g fibre

Tom yums are the most popular soups in Thailand. Translated loosely as broth or stock (tom) and combined spicy sour (yum), this soup is far more than the name would indicate. Sour and tangy, without the sweetness of coconut, tom yum goong's unique taste comes from the combination of spicy ingredients, like chilli and curry paste, with sour ones like lime juice and tamarind.

tom yum goong

900g uncooked large king prawns
1 tablespoon peanut oil
1.5 litres (6 cups) water
2 tablespoons red curry paste
1 tablespoon tamarind concentrate
10cm stick fresh lemon grass (20g), chopped finely
1 teaspoon ground turmeric
2 fresh small red thai chillies, chopped coarsely
1cm piece fresh ginger (5g), grated
6 fresh kaffir lime leaves, shredded finely
1 teaspoon grated palm sugar
100g fresh shiitake mushrooms, halved
2 tablespoons fish sauce
2 tablespoons lime juice
¼ cup loosely packed vietnamese mint leaves
¼ cup loosely packed fresh coriander leaves

When you use fresh lemon grass, chop starting from the white end, going up only until you just reach the green part of the stalk (as if you were cutting a green onion). Discard the tough top green section; cut the white part as finely as possible because lemon grass is so fibrous it doesn't break down in cooking.

1. Shell and devein prawns, leaving tails intact; reserve heads and shells.
2. Heat oil in large saucepan; cook prawn shells and heads, stirring, about 5 minutes or until a deep orange in colour.
3. Add 1 cup of the water and curry paste to pan; bring to a boil, stirring. Add remaining water; return to a boil. Reduce heat; simmer, uncovered, 20 minutes. Strain broth through muslin-lined sieve or colander into large heatproof bowl; discard solids.
4. Return broth to same cleaned pan. Add tamarind, lemon grass, turmeric, chilli, ginger, lime leaf and sugar; bring to a boil. Boil, stirring, 2 minutes. Add mushrooms, reduce heat; cook, stirring, 3 minutes. Add prawns; simmer, uncovered, about 5 minutes or until prawns are cooked as desired. Remove from heat; stir in sauce and juice.
5. Serve bowls of soup sprinkled with mint and coriander.

• **preparation time** 20 minutes **cooking time** 40 minutes **serves** 4
per serving 9g total fat (1.3g saturated fat); 849kJ (203 cal); 3.9g carbohydrate; 25.2g protein; 2.3g fibre

chilli crab laksa

2 uncooked whole mud crabs (1.5kg)
2 tablespoons peanut oil
3 fresh long red chillies, chopped finely
2 cloves garlic, crushed
2cm piece fresh ginger (10g), grated
½ cup (125ml) fish stock
⅔ cup (180g) laksa paste
3¼ cups (800ml) coconut milk
1 litre (4 cups) chicken stock
3 fresh kaffir lime leaves, shredded finely
1 fresh long red chilli, chopped finely, extra
1 tablespoon lime juice
1 tablespoon fish sauce
1 tablespoon grated palm sugar
250g rice stick noodles
3 green onions, sliced thinly
3 cups (240g) bean sprouts
½ cup loosely packed fresh coriander leaves

1 Place crabs in large container filled with ice and water; stand 1 hour. Leaving flesh in claws and legs, prepare crab by lifting tail flap and, with a peeling motion, lift off back shell. Remove and discard whitish gills, liver and brain matter; crack claws with back of knife. Rinse crabs well. Using cleaver or heavy knife, chop each body into quarters; crack large claws lightly with back of knife.

2 Heat oil in wok; stir-fry chilli, garlic and ginger until fragrant. Add crab and fish stock to wok; bring to a boil. Reduce heat; simmer, covered, about 20 minutes or until crab is changed in colour. Discard liquid in wok.

3 Meanwhile, cook paste in large saucepan, stirring, until fragrant. Stir in coconut milk, chicken stock, lime leaf and extra chilli; bring to a boil. Reduce heat; simmer, covered, 20 minutes. Stir in juice, sauce and sugar.

4 Meanwhile, place noodles in large heatproof bowl; cover with boiling water. Stand until tender; drain.

5 Divide noodles and crab among serving bowls; ladle laksa into bowls, top with onion, sprouts and coriander.

• **preparation time** 40 minutes (plus standing time) **cooking time** 30 minutes **serves** 4 **per serving** 68.2g total fat (40g saturated fat); 4088kJ (978 cal); 31.6g carbohydrate; 55.9g protein; 10.8g fibre

mussels in spiced coconut broth

1kg medium black mussels
1 cup (250ml) water
3 cups (750ml) fish stock
10cm piece fresh ginger (50g), sliced thinly
2 fresh small red thai chillies, sliced thinly
4 cloves garlic, sliced thinly
3 dried curry leaves
4 shallots (100g), sliced thinly
1 tablespoon fish sauce
1 teaspoon finely grated lemon rind
2 teaspoons lemon juice
½ cup (125ml) coconut milk
1 cup firmly packed fresh coriander leaves

1   Scrub mussels; remove beards.
2   Place the water and stock in large saucepan with ginger, chilli, garlic, curry leaves, shallot, sauce, rind, juice and milk; bring to a boil. Reduce heat; simmer, covered, 20 minutes.
3   Add mussels; simmer, covered, about 5 minutes or until mussels open (discard any that do not).
4   Serve bowls of soup sprinkled with coriander.
•   **preparation time** 15 minutes **cooking time** 30 minutes **serves** 4
    per serving 8g total fat (6.2g saturated fat); 585kJ (140 cal); 6.7g carbohydrate; 9.7g protein; 1.7g fibre

creamy crab and tomato bisque

4 uncooked medium blue swimmer crabs (1.3kg)
60g butter
1 medium brown onion (150g), chopped coarsely
1 medium carrot (120g), chopped coarsely
1 medium leek (350g), chopped coarsely
2 cloves garlic, crushed
1 tablespoon tomato paste
2 tablespoons brandy
1 cup (250ml) dry white wine
1.25 litres (5 cups) fish stock
1 bay leaf
2 sprigs fresh thyme
2 medium tomatoes (300g), chopped finely
20g butter, extra
1 tablespoon plain flour
½ cup (125ml) cream

We suggest you make your own stock for this recipe; see the recipe on page 113.

1   Slide knife under top of crab shells at back, lever off and discard. Discard gills; rinse crabs under cold water. Using cleaver or heavy knife, chop each body into quarters.
2   Melt butter in large saucepan; cook onion, carrot, leek and garlic, stirring, until vegetables soften. Add crab, in batches; cook, stirring, until changed in colour.
3   Add paste to pan; cook, stirring, 2 minutes. Return crab to pan with brandy; stir over heat about 2 minutes or until alcohol evaporates.
4   Add wine, stock, bay leaf, thyme and tomato; bring to a boil. Reduce heat; simmer, uncovered, 45 minutes.
5   Meanwhile, using back of teaspoon, work extra butter into flour in small bowl.
6   Strain soup through muslin-lined sieve or colander into large heatproof bowl; extract as much meat as possible from crab, add to soup. Discard shells, claws and other solids.
7   Return soup to same cleaned pan; bring to a boil. Stir in flour mixture and cream; stir until soup boils and thickens slightly.
•   **preparation time** 1 hour **cooking time** 1 hour 20 minutes **serves** 4 **per serving** 32g total fat (20.1g saturated fat); 2152kJ (515 cal); 13.1g carbohydrate; 27.1g protein; 4.4g fibre

mediterranean fish

1 tablespoon olive oil
1 clove garlic, crushed
1 small leek (200g), halved, sliced thinly
1 small red capsicum (150g), cut into 1cm pieces
1 small red onion (100g), halved, sliced thinly
1 trimmed celery stalk (100g), cut into 1cm pieces
1 small carrot (70g), cut into 1cm pieces
½ teaspoon finely grated orange rind
¼ teaspoon dried chilli flakes
2 tablespoons tomato paste
2 cups (500ml) water
3 cups (750ml) fish stock
¼ cup (60ml) dry white wine
2 large egg tomatoes (180g), chopped coarsely
200g uncooked small king prawns
200g skinless blue-eye fillet, chopped coarsely
200g skinless ocean trout fillet, chopped coarsely
¼ teaspoon finely chopped fresh thyme
1 tablespoon finely chopped fresh dill

1 Heat oil in large saucepan; cook garlic, leek, capsicum, onion, celery, carrot, rind and chilli, stirring, until vegetables soften.
2 Add paste, the water, stock, wine and tomato; bring to a boil. Reduce heat; simmer, uncovered, 20 minutes.
3 Meanwhile, shell and devein prawns; chop meat coarsely. Add prawn meat, fish, thyme and half the dill to soup; simmer, uncovered, about 3 minutes or until prawn and fish are cooked.
4 Serve bowls of soup sprinkled with remaining dill.
• **preparation time** 25 minutes **cooking time** 30 minutes **serves** 4
per serving 7.7g total fat (1.4g saturated fat); 978kJ (234 cal); 8.5g carbohydrate; 28.3g protein; 3.7g fibre

thai salmon broth with sesame sticky rice patties

2 cups (500ml) water
3 cups (750ml) fish stock
3 x 10cm sticks fresh lemon grass (60g), bruised
3 fresh kaffir lime leaves, torn
1 fresh long red chilli, sliced thinly
2cm piece fresh ginger (10g), grated
440g skinless salmon fillets
1 tablespoon fish sauce
2 tablespoons lime juice
150g snow peas, halved crossways
230g can sliced bamboo shoots, rinsed, drained
3 green onions, sliced thinly
sesame sticky rice patties
1 cup (200g) glutinous rice
1 tablespoon toasted black sesame seeds
1½ tablespoons rice wine vinegar

We suggest you make your own stock for this recipe; see the recipe on page 113.

1 Cover rice for sesame sticky rice patties with water; stand overnight.
2 Make sesame sticky rice patties.
3 Meanwhile, place the water and stock in large saucepan with lemon grass, lime leaf, chilli and ginger; bring to a boil. Reduce heat; simmer, uncovered, 10 minutes.
4 Add fish to pan; simmer, uncovered, about 10 minutes or until cooked as desired. Transfer fish to medium bowl; using fork, flake into small pieces.
5 Stir sauce, juice, snow peas and bamboo shoots into soup; simmer, uncovered, about 2 minutes or until snow peas are just tender. Discard lemon grass.
6 Divide fish and rice patties among serving bowls; ladle soup into bowls, sprinkle with onion.

sesame sticky rice patties Drain rice; rinse well under cold water, drain. Place rice in steamer lined with muslin or cloth. Place steamer over saucepan of boiling water, cover tightly; steam about 20 minutes or until rice is tender. Combine rice in medium bowl with seeds and vinegar; roll level tablespoons of rice mixture into balls. Gently flatten balls, place on tray; cover with damp tea towel until required.

• **preparation time** 20 minutes (plus standing time) **cooking time** 30 minutes **serves** 4
per serving 10.3g total fat (2.2g saturated fat); 402kJ (176 cal); 44.7g carbohydrate; 30.4g protein; 2.9g fibre

Poultry

duck and mushroom

20g dried shiitake mushrooms
15g dried black fungus
1kg chinese barbecued duck
1 litre (4 cups) water
1 litre (4 cups) chicken stock
2 teaspoons grated palm sugar
1 tablespoon mushroom soy sauce
230g can bamboo shoots, rinsed, drained
100g swiss brown mushrooms, sliced thinly
1 tablespoon cornflour
1 tablespoon water, extra
4 green onions, sliced thinly

1 Cover dried mushrooms in small bowl with cold water; stand 1 hour. Drain; slice thinly.
2 Meanwhile, remove bones from duck; reserve skin, slice meat thinly.
3 Preheat grill.
4 Combine the water and stock in large saucepan; bring to a boil. Add duck, dried mushrooms, sugar, sauce, bamboo shoots and swiss browns; return to a boil.
5 Place duck skin, in single layer, on oven tray; grill about 5 minutes or until crisp. Discard excess fat; chop skin coarsely.
6 Meanwhile, add blended cornflour and extra water to soup; stir until mixture thickens slightly. Serve soup sprinkled with duck skin and onion.
• **preparation time** 10 minutes (plus standing time) **cooking time** 30 minutes **serves** 6
per serving 22.4g total fat (6.8g saturated fat); 1246kJ (298 cal);
4.7g carbohydrate; 19.5g protein; 1.1g fibre

Also known as risi, risoni is a very small, rice-shaped pasta similar to orzo that is often used by Italian cooks when making soup. It can also be baked in a casserole or served as a side dish to a rich meaty main course.

chicken and risoni with herbed meatballs

2.5 litres (10 cups) water
1.6kg whole chicken
1 large tomato (220g), halved
2 trimmed celery stalks (200g), halved
1 medium brown onion (150g), halved
2 fresh flat-leaf parsley stalks
5 black peppercorns
300g chicken mince
½ cup (50g) packaged breadcrumbs
2 tablespoons finely chopped fresh flat-leaf parsley
2 tablespoons finely grated parmesan cheese
1 egg
1 tablespoon olive oil
¾ cup (165g) risoni
2 tablespoons lemon juice
⅓ cup coarsely chopped fresh flat-leaf parsley

1 Place the water in large saucepan with whole chicken, tomato, celery, onion, parsley stalks and peppercorns; bring to a boil. Reduce heat; simmer, covered, 2 hours.

2 Remove chicken from pan. Strain broth through muslin-lined sieve or colander into large heatproof bowl; discard solids. Allow broth to cool, cover; refrigerate overnight. When chicken is cool enough to handle, remove and discard skin and bones. Shred meat coarsely; cover, refrigerate overnight.

3 Combine mince, breadcrumbs, finely chopped parsley, cheese and egg in medium bowl; roll rounded teaspoons of mixture into balls. Heat oil in medium saucepan; cook meatballs, in batches, until browned all over.

4 Skim and discard fat from surface of broth. Return broth to large saucepan; bring to a boil. Reduce heat; simmer, uncovered, 20 minutes. Add meatballs and pasta; simmer, uncovered, about 10 minutes or until meatballs are cooked through and pasta is just tender. Add 2 cups of the reserved chicken (keep remaining chicken for another use), juice and coarsely chopped parsley to pan; stir soup over medium heat until hot.

• **preparation time** 30 minutes (plus refrigeration time) **cooking time** 2 hours 45 minutes **serves** 4 **per serving** 45.8g total fat (3.7g saturated fat); 3536kJ (846 cal); 40.4g carbohydrate; 66.3g protein; 4.3g fibre

duck and lentil

1.8kg whole duck
1.5 litres (6 cups) water
1 litre (4 cups) chicken stock
2 teaspoons olive oil
6 slices pancetta (90g), chopped finely
2 medium carrots (240g), diced into 1cm pieces
2 trimmed celery stalks (200g), diced into 1cm pieces
1 medium leek (350g), sliced thinly
2 teaspoons black mustard seeds
¾ cup (150g) french green lentils

French green lentils hold their shape particularly well during cooking and do not require any pre-soaking before use.

1   Preheat oven to 200°C/180°C fan-forced.
2   Wash duck under cold water; pat dry inside and out with absorbent paper.
3   Tuck wings under duck. Place duck, breast-side up, on wire rack in large baking dish. Prick duck skin with fork several times. Roast, uncovered, about 1½ hours or until cooked through. When cool enough to handle, remove and discard skin from duck; shred meat. Chop bones into large pieces.
4   Combine bones in large saucepan with the water and stock; bring to a boil. Reduce heat; simmer, uncovered, 35 minutes, skimming fat from surface occasionally. Strain broth through muslin-lined sieve or colander into large heatproof bowl; discard solids.
5   Heat oil in same cleaned pan; cook pancetta, carrot, celery and leek, stirring, about 5 minutes or until vegetables just soften. Add seeds and lentils; cook, stirring, 2 minutes. Add broth and duck meat; bring to a boil. Reduce heat; simmer, uncovered, about 25 minutes or until lentils are tender.

•   **preparation time** 45 minutes **cooking time** 3 hours **serves** 6
    per serving 60.3g total fat (18.1g saturated fat); 3060kJ (732 cal); 14.6g carbohydrate; 31.5g protein; 6.2g fibre

Aromatic fresh kaffir lime leaves are used similarly to bay or curry leaves in the food of South-East Asia. Sold fresh, dried or frozen, they look like two glossy dark-green leaves joined end to end, forming a rounded hourglass shape. While readily available in most greengrocers and many supermarkets, you can use washed lemon or lime tree leaves instead, but the finished soup will lack their distinctive pungent sharpness.

coconut, chicken and kaffir lime

1 tablespoon peanut oil
600g chicken thigh fillets, cut into 1cm strips
¼ cup (75g) green curry paste
1 litre (4 cups) chicken stock
3¼ cups (800ml) coconut milk
1 long green chilli, chopped finely
8 fresh kaffir lime leaves, shredded
125g rice vermicelli
2 tablespoons grated palm sugar
2 tablespoons lime juice
2 tablespoons fish sauce
1 cup (80g) bean sprouts
½ cup loosely packed vietnamese mint leaves
1 long green chilli, sliced thinly
2 limes, cut into thin wedges

1   Heat oil in large saucepan; cook chicken, in batches, until browned lightly.
2   Place paste in same pan; cook, stirring, until fragrant. Return chicken to pan with stock, coconut milk, chopped chilli and lime leaf; bring to a boil. Reduce heat; simmer, uncovered, 30 minutes, skimming fat from surface occasionally. Add vermicelli; cook, uncovered, until vermicelli is just tender. Stir in sugar, juice and sauce.
3   Serve soup sprinkled with sprouts, mint, sliced chilli and lime.
•   **preparation time** 15 minutes **cooking time** 45 minutes **serves** 4
     per serving 63.9g total fat (41.6g saturated fat); 3478kJ (832 cal); 25g carbohydrate; 38g protein; 6.8g fibre

Tom (broth or stock), ka (fresh galangal) and gai (chicken) come together in this popular Thai soup that is more subtle and smoother than its fiery counterpart, tom yum goong, thanks to the moderating effect of the added coconut milk.

tom ka gai

1 litre (4 cups) chicken stock
4cm piece fresh galangal (20g), sliced thinly
2 x 10cm sticks fresh lemon grass (40g), cut into 5cm pieces
2 fresh kaffir lime leaves
2 teaspoons coarsely chopped coriander root and stem
500g chicken thigh fillets, sliced thinly
200g canned straw mushrooms, rinsed, drained
1 cup (250ml) coconut milk
1 tablespoon lime juice
1 tablespoon fish sauce
1 teaspoon grated palm sugar
¼ cup loosely packed fresh coriander leaves
2 fresh small red thai chillies, sliced thinly
2 fresh kaffir lime leaves, shredded finely
10cm stick fresh lemon grass (20g), sliced thinly

Leftover coconut milk should be refrigerated; it will keep for up to a week. We do not suggest freezing leftover coconut milk because it increases the likelihood of curdling when the thawed milk is used in cooking. Avoid buying cans of sweetened coconut milk as it's not the right ingredient for use in Thai cooking.

1 Combine stock in large saucepan with galangal, lemon grass pieces, whole lime leaves and coriander root and stem mixture; bring to a boil. Reduce heat; simmer, covered, 5 minutes. Remove from heat; stand 10 minutes. Strain broth through muslin-lined sieve or colander into large heatproof bowl; discard solids.

2 Return broth to same cleaned pan. Add chicken and mushrooms; bring to a boil. Reduce heat; simmer, uncovered, about 5 minutes or until chicken is cooked through. Stir in coconut milk, juice, sauce and sugar; cook, stirring, until hot (do not allow to boil). Remove from heat; stir in coriander leaves, chilli, shredded lime leaf and sliced lemon grass.

• preparation time 15 minutes cooking time 35 minutes serves 4
per serving 21.1g total fat (14.6g saturated fat); 1455kJ (348 cal); 5.6g carbohydrate; 28.9g protein; 2.5g fibre

This soup is our take on the classic Greek avgolemono (which translates as egg and lemon). There are as many variations of this soup as there are Greek families, but the avgolemono mixture, added near the end of the cooking time, is always the crowning glory.

chicken, lemon and rice

2 teaspoons olive oil
1 small brown onion (80g), chopped finely
1 litre (4 cups) chicken stock
400g chicken breast fillets, chopped coarsely
⅓ cup (65g) white short-grain rice
2 eggs
⅓ cup (80ml) lemon juice
2 tablespoons finely chopped fresh flat-leaf parsley

We suggest you make your own stock for this recipe; see the recipe on page 112. Arborio rice, otherwise known as white short-grain rice, is an excellent choice for this recipe due to its high starch level, making for a deliciously creamy soup.

1   Heat oil in large saucepan; cook onion, stirring, until soft. Add stock, chicken and rice; bring to a boil. Reduce heat; simmer, covered, about 20 minutes or until rice is tender.
2   Whisk eggs and juice in small bowl until smooth. Gradually whisk ½ cup hot soup into egg mixture then stir warmed egg mixture into soup.
3   Serve bowls of soup sprinkled with parsley.
•   **preparation time** 10 minutes **cooking time** 35 minutes **serves** 4
   per serving 8.4g total fat (2.3g saturated fat); 1099kJ (263 cal); 16.3g carbohydrate; 30.3g protein; 0.5g fibre

Gumbo, an African word for okra, is basically any Cajun soup thickened with a roux (a flour/butter mix), its specific content left up to the individual, but usually including rice and sausage. Okra, introduced to creole-cajun cooking by African slaves brought to Louisiana, is a distinctively textured green vegetable most often used in casseroles, stews and soups.

chicken, chorizo and okra gumbo

3 litres (12 cups) water
1.5kg whole chicken
2 medium carrots (240g), chopped coarsely
2 trimmed celery stalks (200g), chopped coarsely
1 medium brown onion (150g), chopped coarsely
12 black peppercorns
1 bay leaf
60g butter
1 small brown onion (80g), chopped finely, extra
2 cloves garlic, crushed
1 medium red capsicum (200g), chopped finely
2 teaspoons dried oregano
1 teaspoon sweet paprika
¼ teaspoon cayenne pepper
¼ teaspoon ground clove
¼ cup (35g) plain flour
¼ cup (70g) tomato paste
400g can crushed tomatoes
100g fresh okra, halved diagonally
1 cup (200g) calrose rice
1 chorizo sausage (170g), sliced thinly

If you want to cook this gumbo a day ahead, the flavours will meld and deepen, making the soup even more delicious. Follow the recipe through to the end of step 2 then cool the soup, cover and refrigerate it overnight.

1 Place the water in large saucepan with chicken, carrot, celery, onion, peppercorns and bay leaf; bring to a boil. Reduce heat; simmer, covered, 1½ hours.

2 Remove chicken from pan. Strain broth through muslin-lined sieve or colander into large heatproof bowl; discard solids. When chicken is cool enough to handle, remove and discard skin and bones; shred meat coarsely.

3 Melt butter in large saucepan; cook extra onion and garlic, stirring, until onion softens. Add capsicum, herbs and spices; cook, stirring, until mixture is fragrant. Add flour and paste; cook, stirring, 1 minute. Gradually stir in reserved broth and undrained tomatoes; bring to a boil, stirring. Stir in okra and rice, reduce heat; simmer, uncovered, about 15 minutes, stirring occasionally, or until rice is tender.

4 Meanwhile, heat large oiled frying pan; cook sausage until browned; drain. Add sausage with chicken to gumbo; stir over medium heat until hot.

• **preparation time** 30 minutes **cooking time** 2 hours 45 minutes **serves** 8
per serving 26.8g total fat (5.7g saturated fat); 2011kJ (481 cal); 30.5g carbohydrate; 27.8g protein; 3.9g fibre

cantonese chicken dumpling

10 dried shiitake mushrooms
2 teaspoons peanut oil
2 cloves garlic, crushed
2cm piece fresh ginger (10g), grated
1 litre (4 cups) water
1 litre (4 cups) chicken stock
2 tablespoons dark soy sauce
200g baby corn, halved lengthways
150g bean sprouts
3 green onions, sliced thinly

The chicken dumpling mixture makes 40 dumplings so you need a package containing at least 40 wonton wrappers. You can make the dumplings whenever you like, and freeze them, separated in two, or even four, batches, sealed tightly in snap-lock bags. When you want to use them, remove what you need from the freezer and pop them into the soup. They do not need defrosting first, but make sure that they are cooked through before serving.

1 Cover mushrooms with ½ cup cold water in small bowl; stand 15 minutes. Drain over small bowl; reserve soaking liquid. Slice mushrooms thinly.

2 Meanwhile, make chicken dumplings.

3 Heat oil in large saucepan; cook garlic and ginger, stirring, 2 minutes. Stir in the water, stock, sauce and reserved soaking liquid; bring to a boil. Reduce heat; simmer, uncovered, 15 minutes.

4 Add mushrooms, dumplings and corn to soup; bring to a boil. Reduce heat; simmer, about 10 minutes or until dumplings are cooked through.

5 Serve bowls of soup sprinkled with sprouts and onion.

• **preparation time** 25 minutes (plus standing time) **cooking time** 30 minutes **serves** 4 **per serving** 4.1g total fat (1g saturated fat); 518kJ (124 cal); 12.4g carbohydrate; 7.4g protein; 4.7g fibre

accompaniment

chicken dumplings

Heat 1 tablespoon of peanut oil in medium frying pan; add 2 thinly sliced green onions, 3cm piece grated fresh ginger and 1 finely chopped fresh long red chilli to pan. Cook, stirring, until onion softens. Add 300g chicken mince; cook, stirring, until browned. Stir in 2 teaspoons dark soy sauce; cool. Place rounded teaspoon of mince mixture in centre of each wonton wrapper; brush around edges with a little water, gather edges around filling, pinch together to seal. Use half the wontons for soup; freeze remainder, sealed tightly, for future use.

serves 4 **per serving** 5.8g total fat (1.4g saturated fat); 803kJ (192 cal); 22.7g carbohydrate; 11.7g protein; 0.1g fibre

cream of chicken with herb and cheese damper

2 litres (8 cups) water
1 litre (4 cups) chicken stock
1.8kg whole chicken
1 medium carrot (120g), chopped coarsely
1 trimmed celery stalk (100g), chopped coarsely
1 medium brown onion (150g), chopped coarsely
40g butter
⅓ cup (50g) plain flour
2 tablespoons lemon juice
½ cup (125ml) cream
¼ cup finely chopped fresh flat-leaf parsley

1 Place the water and stock in large saucepan with chicken, carrot, celery and onion; bring to a boil. Reduce heat; simmer, covered, 1½ hours. Remove chicken from pan; simmer broth, covered, 30 minutes.

2 Strain broth through muslin-lined sieve or colander into large heatproof bowl; discard solids. Remove and discard chicken skin and bones; shred meat coarsely.

3 Preheat oven to 200°C/180°C fan-forced. Make herb and cheese damper.

4 Melt butter in large saucepan, add flour; cook, stirring, until mixture thickens and bubbles. Gradually stir in broth and juice; bring to a boil, stirring. Add cream, reduce heat; simmer, uncovered, about 25 minutes, stirring occasionally. Add chicken; stir soup over medium heat until hot.

5 Serve bowls of soup sprinkled with parsley, accompanied with damper.

• **preparation time** 35 minutes **cooking time** 2 hours 30 minutes **serves** 4
per serving 58.6g total fat (14.9g saturated fat); 3327kJ (796 cal); 15.5g carbohydrate; 51.9g protein; 2.4g fibre

accompaniment

herb and cheese damper
Heat 2 teaspoons olive oil in small saucepan; cook 1 finely chopped small brown onion, stirring, until soft. Cool 5 minutes. Place 1⅓ cups self-raising flour in medium bowl; add onion, ⅓ cup coarsely grated cheddar cheese and 2 tablespoons each finely chopped fresh flat-leaf parsley and chives. Stir in as much of ⅔ cup milk required to mix to a soft, sticky dough. Turn dough onto floured surface; knead until smooth. Divide dough into four pieces, shape into rounds. Place on oiled oven tray; sprinkle with 2 tablespoons coarsely grated parmesan cheese. Bake about 20 minutes or until browned lightly.
serves 4 **per serving** 8.9g total fat (4.3g saturated fat); 1133kJ (271 cal); 36.2g carbohydrate; 10.2g protein; 2.3g fibre

Meat Soup

beefy black-eyed bean and spinach

1 cup (200g) black-eyed beans
1 tablespoon olive oil
1 medium brown onion (150g), chopped finely
1 clove garlic, crushed
2.5 litres beef stock (10 cups)
¼ cup (60ml) dry red wine
2 tablespoons tomato paste
500g piece beef skirt steak
250g trimmed spinach, chopped coarsely

We suggest you make your own stock for this recipe; see the recipe on page 112. You need 1kg of untrimmed spinach to get the amount of trimmed spinach required for this recipe.

1   Place beans in medium bowl, cover with water, stand overnight, drain. Rinse under cold water; drain.
2   Heat oil in large saucepan; cook onion and garlic, stirring, until onion softens. Add stock, wine, paste and beef to pan; bring to a boil. Reduce heat; simmer, covered, 40 minutes. Uncover; simmer 30 minutes.
3   Remove beef from pan. Add beans to pan; bring to a boil. Reduce heat; simmer, uncovered, until beans are tender.
4   Meanwhile, when beef is cool enough to handle, remove and discard fat and sinew. Chop beef coarsely; return to pan with spinach; simmer, uncovered, until soup is hot.
•   **preparation time** 5 minutes (plus standing time) **cooking time** 1 hour 50 minutes **serves** 4 **per serving** 13.9g total fat (4.2g saturated fat); 2199kJ (526 cal); 28.3g carbohydrate; 62.6g protein; 12.4g fibre

Merguez, the French spelling of the Arabic "mirqaz", is a small spicy lamb sausage eaten in Tunisia and Algeria. It is served grilled as part of a mezze, or fried then cooked with pulses, various meats and vegetables in tagines, cassoulet or other hearty casseroles.

bean and merguez with gremolata

1 medium red onion (170g), chopped coarsely
2 rindless bacon rashers (130g), chopped coarsely
2 cloves garlic, crushed
400g can diced tomatoes
1.5 litres (6 cups) chicken stock
6 merguez sausages (480g)
2 x 400g cans white beans, rinsed, drained
gremolata
⅓ cup finely chopped fresh flat-leaf parsley
2 teaspoons finely grated lemon rind
2 cloves garlic, crushed

We suggest you make your own stock for this recipe; see the recipe on page 112.

1 Cook onion, bacon and garlic in heated oiled large saucepan, stirring, until onion softens and bacon crisps. Add undrained tomatoes and stock; bring to a boil. Reduce heat; simmer, uncovered, 20 minutes, stirring occasionally.

2 Meanwhile, cook sausages in heated oiled medium frying pan until browned and cooked through; slice thinly.

3 Add sausage to soup with beans; stir until soup is hot.

4 Serve bowls of soup sprinkled with gremolata.

gremolata Combine ingredients in a small bowl.

• **preparation time** 10 minutes **cooking time** 40 minutes **serves** 4
per serving 42.4g total fat (15.6g saturated fat); 2504kJ (599 cal); 14.6g carbohydrate; 38.4g protein; 5.5g fibre

Chinese barbecued pork is roasted pork fillet with a sweet, sticky coating. It is available from Asian grocery stores or specialty food shops.

barbecued pork in orange and tamarind broth

20g dried shiitake mushrooms
2 teaspoons vegetable oil
4 shallots (100g), chopped finely
1 clove garlic, crushed
2 fresh small red thai chillies, chopped finely
2 litres (8 cups) water
1 litre (4 cups) beef stock
2 teaspoons finely grated orange rind
¼ cup (60ml) orange juice
1 tablespoon tamarind concentrate
400g chinese barbecued pork, sliced thinly
100g swiss brown mushrooms, sliced thinly
4 green onions, sliced thinly

1   Place dried mushrooms in small bowl, cover with cold water; stand 1 hour. Drain; remove stems, slice thinly.
2   Meanwhile, heat oil in large saucepan; cook shallot, garlic and chilli, stirring, until shallot softens. Add the water, stock, rind, juice and tamarind; bring to a boil. Add pork, sliced dried mushrooms and swiss browns; reduce heat, simmer, covered, about 10 minutes or until soup is hot.
3   Serve bowls of soup sprinkled with onion.
•   **preparation time** 15 minutes (plus standing time) **cooking time** 30 minutes **serves** 8 **per serving** 9.1g total fat (3.4g saturated fat); 648kJ (155 cal); 4.3g carbohydrate; 13.1g protein; 2.1g fibre

Large bowls of pho are a breakfast favourite throughout Vietnam, but we like to eat it any time of the day. Round steak, skirt steak and gravy beef are also suitable for this recipe, but the cooking times will change depending on which cut is used.

vietnamese beef pho

2 litres (8 cups) water
1 litre (4 cups) beef stock
1kg chuck steak
2 star anise
8cm piece fresh ginger (40g), grated
⅓ cup (80ml) japanese soy sauce
200g bean thread noodles
1½ cups (120g) bean sprouts
¼ cup loosely packed fresh coriander leaves
⅓ cup loosely packed fresh mint leaves
4 green onions, sliced thinly
2 fresh long red chillies, sliced thinly
¼ cup (60ml) fish sauce
1 medium lemon (140g), cut into 6 wedges

1 Place the water and stock in large saucepan with beef, star anise, ginger and soy sauce; bring to a boil. Reduce heat; simmer, covered, 30 minutes. Uncover, simmer about 30 minutes or until beef is tender.

2 Meanwhile, place noodles in medium heatproof bowl, cover with boiling water; stand until just tender, drain. Combine sprouts, coriander, mint, onion and chilli in medium bowl.

3 Remove beef from pan. Strain broth through muslin-lined sieve or colander into large heatproof bowl; discard solids. When beef is cool enough to handle, remove and discard fat and sinew. Slice beef thinly, return to same cleaned pan with broth; bring to a boil. Stir in fish sauce.

4 Divide noodles among soup bowls; ladle hot beef broth into bowls, sprinkle with sprout mixture, serve with lemon.

• **preparation time** 20 minutes **cooking time** 1 hour 20 minutes **serves** 6 **per serving** 8g total fat (3.3g saturated fat); 1166kJ (279 cal); 11.8g carbohydrate; 38.3g protein; 2.4g fibre

scotch broth with cheese scones

2.25 litres (9 cups) water
1kg lamb neck chops
¾ cup (150g) pearl barley
1 large brown onion (200g), diced into 1cm pieces
2 medium carrots (240g), diced into 1cm pieces
1 medium leek (350g), sliced thinly
2 cups (160g) finely shredded savoy cabbage
½ cup (60g) frozen peas
2 tablespoons coarsely chopped fresh flat-leaf parsley

1   Place the water in large saucepan with lamb and barley; bring to a boil. Reduce heat; simmer, covered, 1 hour, skimming fat from surface occasionally. Add onion, carrot and leek; simmer, covered, about 30 minutes or until carrot is tender.
2   Meanwhile, make cheese scones.
3   Remove lamb from pan. When cool enough to handle, remove and discard bones; shred lamb coarsely.
4   Return lamb to soup with cabbage and peas; cook, uncovered, about 10 minutes or until cabbage is just tender.
5   Serve bowls of soup sprinkled with parsley, and accompanied with scones.
•   **preparation time** 30 minutes **cooking time** 1 hour 45 minutes **serves** 4
    per serving 24.4g total fat (10.7g saturated fat); 2274kJ (544 cal); 32.8g carbohydrate; 43.2g protein; 10.7g fibre

accompaniment

cheese scones
Preheat oven to 220°C/200°C fan-forced. Lightly grease and flour 8cm x 26cm bar pan. Combine 1 cup self-raising flour, a pinch of cayenne pepper, 2 tablespoons finely grated parmesan cheese and ¼ cup coarsely grated cheddar cheese in medium bowl; pour in ½ cup milk, stir until mixture forms a sticky dough. Gently knead dough on floured surface until smooth; use hand to flatten dough to 2cm-thickness. Using 4.5cm cutter, cut rounds from dough; place rounds, slightly touching, in pan. Brush scones with a little milk then sprinkle with ¼ cup coarsely grated cheddar cheese. Bake about 20 minutes.
serves 4 **per serving** 7.8g total fat (4.8g saturated fat); 907kJ (217 cal); 26.2g carbohydrate; 9.6g protein; 1.3g fibre

beef and barley

1 tablespoon olive oil
500g gravy beef, trimmed, diced into 2cm pieces
2 cloves garlic, crushed
2 medium brown onions (300g), chopped finely
¾ cup (150g) pearl barley
3 cups (750ml) beef stock
1.5 litres (6 cups) water
1 bay leaf
1 sprig fresh rosemary
1 sprig fresh thyme
2 medium potatoes (400g), diced into 1cm pieces
2 medium carrots (240g), diced into 1cm pieces
2 medium zucchini (240g), diced into 1cm pieces
2 medium yellow patty-pan squash (60g), diced into 1cm pieces
100g swiss brown mushrooms, chopped coarsely
½ cup finely chopped fresh flat-leaf parsley

We suggest you make your own stock for this recipe; see the recipe on page 112.

1 Heat half the oil in large saucepan; cook beef, in batches, until browned.

2 Heat remaining oil in same pan; cook garlic and onion, stirring, until onion softens. Return beef to pan with barley, stock, the water, bay leaf, rosemary and thyme, bring to a boil. Reduce heat; simmer, covered, about 1 hour or until beef and barley are tender, skimming fat occasionally.

3 Add potato, carrot, zucchini, squash and mushrooms to soup; simmer, covered, about 25 minutes or until vegetables are softened. Remove and discard bay leaf, rosemary and thyme.

4 Serve bowls of soup sprinkled with parsley.

• **preparation time** 30 minutes **cooking time** 1 hour 45 minutes **serves** 6
per serving 8.8g total fat (2.6g saturated fat); 1350kJ (323 cal);
30g carbohydrate; 26.9g protein; 7.8g fibre

creamy semi-dried tomato and veal

1 litre (4 cups) water
500g piece boneless veal shoulder
6 black peppercorns
1 bay leaf
60g butter
1 medium brown onion (150g), chopped coarsely
1 clove garlic, crushed
⅓ cup (50g) plain flour
6 large egg tomatoes (540g), chopped coarsely
2 tablespoons tomato paste
½ cup (125ml) cream
⅓ cup (75g) semi-dried tomatoes, drained, chopped finely
2 tablespoons finely shredded fresh basil

1 Place the water in large saucepan with veal, peppercorns and bay leaf; bring to a boil. Reduce heat; simmer, covered, about 1½ hours or until veal is tender.
2 Transfer veal to medium bowl; using two forks, shred veal coarsely. Strain broth through muslin-lined sieve or colander into large heatproof bowl; discard solids.
3 Melt butter in large saucepan; cook onion and garlic, stirring, until onion softens. Add flour; cook, stirring, until mixture thickens and bubbles. Gradually stir in broth; stir over medium heat until soup boils and thickens slightly. Add egg tomato and paste; return to a boil. Reduce heat; simmer, covered, 10 minutes. Cool 15 minutes.
4 Meanwhile, make toasted ciabatta with basil butter.
5 Blend or process soup, in batches, until smooth. Return soup to same cleaned pan, add cream; stir over medium heat until hot.
6 Serve bowls of soup topped with shredded veal and semi-dried tomato, sprinkled with shredded basil and accompanied with toasted ciabatta with basil butter.
• **preparation time** 30 minutes **cooking time** 2 hours **serves** 6
   per serving 20.1g total fat (12g saturated fat); 1430kJ (342 cal); 15.3g carbohydrate; 23.2g protein; 4.2g fibre

accompaniment

toasted ciabatta with basil butter
Combine 50g softened butter with 1 tablespoon finely chopped basil in small bowl. Toast 8 thick slices ciabatta, both sides; spread with basil butter.
serves 6 **per serving** 8.1g total fat (4.6g saturated fat); 660kJ (158 cal); 17.7g carbohydrate; 3.1g protein; 1.2g fibre

mexican bean and shredded pork

2 litres (8 cups) water
2 litres (8 cups) chicken stock
1 large carrot (180g), chopped coarsely
1 trimmed celery stalk (100g), chopped coarsely
5 cloves garlic, unpeeled, bruised
6 black peppercorns
3 sprigs fresh oregano
1 bay leaf
1kg piece pork neck
1 tablespoon olive oil
1 large red onion (300g), chopped coarsely
1 medium red capsicum (200g), chopped coarsely
1 medium yellow capsicum (200g), chopped coarsely
2 fresh long red chillies, sliced thinly
2 cloves garlic, crushed
810g can crushed tomatoes
1 teaspoon ground cumin
2 tablespoons coarsely chopped fresh oregano
420g can kidney beans, rinsed, drained

We suggest you make your own stock for this recipe; see the recipe on page 112.

1   Place the water and stock in large saucepan with carrot, celery, bruised garlic, peppercorns, oregano sprigs, bay leaf and pork; bring to a boil. Reduce heat; simmer, covered, 1 hour. Uncover; simmer 1 hour.

2   Transfer pork to medium bowl; using two forks, shred pork coarsely. Strain broth through muslin-lined sieve or colander into large heatproof bowl; discard solids.

3   Heat oil in same cleaned pan; cook onion, capsicums, chilli and crushed garlic, stirring, until vegetables soften. Return pork and broth to pan with undrained tomatoes, cumin and the chopped oregano; bring to a boil. Reduce heat; simmer, covered, 15 minutes. Add beans; simmer, covered, until soup is hot.

•   **preparation time** 25 minutes **cooking time** 2 hours 30 minutes **serves** 6
    per serving 7.4g total fat (1.6g saturated fat); 1490kJ (356 cal); 20.8g carbohydrate; 46.5g protein; 9.1g fibre

slow-cooked lamb and white bean

1 cup (200g) dried cannellini beans
2 medium red capsicums (400g)
1 tablespoon olive oil
1.5kg french-trimmed lamb shanks
1 large brown onion (200g), chopped coarsely
2 cloves garlic, quartered
2 medium carrots (240g), chopped coarsely
2 trimmed celery stalks (200g), chopped coarsely
2 tablespoons tomato paste
1 cup (250ml) dry red wine
3 litres (12 cups) water
80g baby spinach leaves

1   Place beans in medium bowl, cover with water, stand overnight; drain. Rinse under cold water; drain.
2   Quarter capsicums; discard seeds and membranes. Roast under grill or in very hot oven, skin-side up, until skin blisters and blackens. Cover capsicum pieces with plastic or paper for 5 minutes; peel away skin, dice capsicum finely.
3   Heat oil in large saucepan; cook lamb, in batches, until browned all over. Cook onion and garlic in same pan, stirring, until onion softens. Add carrot and celery; cook, stirring, 2 minutes. Add paste and wine; bring to a boil. Reduce heat; simmer, uncovered, 5 minutes.
4   Return lamb to pan with the water; bring to a boil. Reduce heat; simmer, uncovered, 2 hours, skimming fat from surface occasionally.
5   Meanwhile, place beans in medium saucepan of boiling water; return to a boil. Reduce heat; simmer, uncovered, about 30 minutes or until beans are almost tender. Drain.
6   Remove lamb from pan. Strain broth through muslin-lined sieve or colander into large heatproof bowl; discard solids. When lamb is cool enough to handle, remove meat from shanks; shred coarsely. Discard bones.
7   Return broth to same cleaned pan with capsicum, beans and lamb; bring to a boil. Reduce heat; simmer, uncovered, 5 minutes. Remove from heat; stir in spinach.
•   **preparation time** 35 minutes (plus standing time) **cooking time** 3 hours 20 minutes **serves** 4   **per serving** 1.8g total fat (0.7g saturated fat); 171kJ (41 cal); 1.4g carbohydrate; 3.8g protein; 0.7g fibre

hungarian goulash

2 tablespoons olive oil
40g butter
900g boneless veal shoulder, diced into 2cm pieces
2 medium brown onions (300g), chopped finely
1 tablespoon tomato paste
1 tablespoon plain flour
1 tablespoon sweet paprika
2 teaspoons caraway seeds
½ teaspoon cayenne pepper
2 cloves garlic, crushed
2 cups (500ml) water
1.5 litres (6 cups) beef stock
400g can crushed tomatoes
1 large red capsicum (350g), chopped coarsely
1 medium potato (200g), chopped coarsely
spätzle
1 cup (150g) plain flour
2 eggs, beaten lightly
¼ cup (60ml) water
½ teaspoon cracked black pepper

Spätzle, served throughout Austria, Germany, Switzerland and the French region of Alsace, are tiny noodle-like dumplings made by pushing a batter through the holes of a colander or strainer into a pan of boiling water or stock. The cooked spätzle are generally tossed in a frying pan with melted butter before being served. We suggest you make your own stock for this recipe; see the recipe on page 112.

1 Heat half the oil and half the butter in large saucepan; cook veal, in batches, until browned all over.

2 Heat remaining oil and remaining butter in same pan; cook onion, stirring, about 5 minutes or until onion is slightly caramelised.

3 Add paste, flour, paprika, seeds, cayenne and garlic; cook, stirring, 2 minutes. Return veal to pan with the water, stock and undrained tomatoes; bring to a boil. Reduce heat; simmer, uncovered, 1½ hours. Add capsicum and potato; simmer, uncovered, about 10 minutes or until potato is tender.

4 Meanwhile, make spätzle.

5 Serve bowls of soup topped with spätzle.

spätzle Place flour in small bowl, make well in centre. Gradually add combined egg and the water, stirring, until batter is smooth; stir in pepper. Pour batter into metal colander set over large saucepan of boiling water; using a wooden spoon, push batter through holes of colander. Bring water back to a boil; boil, uncovered, about 2 minutes or until spätzle float to the surface. Use a slotted spoon to remove spätzle; drain before adding to goulash soup.

• **preparation time** 25 minutes **cooking time** 2 hours **serves** 4
per serving 27.3g total fat (9.5g saturated fat); 3022kJ (723 cal); 48g carbohydrate; 68.8g protein; 5.8g fibre

After sundown during Ramadan, many of the Muslims in Morocco break the day's fast by starting their meal with this hearty, nourishing soup. Recipes vary from family to family, but chickpeas and lamb always feature.

harira

1 cup (200g) dried chickpeas
20g butter
2 medium brown onions (300g), chopped finely
2 trimmed celery stalks (200g), chopped finely
2 cloves garlic, crushed
4cm piece fresh ginger (20g), grated
1 teaspoon ground cinnamon
½ teaspoon ground black pepper
pinch saffron threads
500g diced lamb
3 large tomatoes (660g), seeded, chopped coarsely
2 litres (8 cups) hot water
½ cup (100g) brown lentils
2 tablespoons plain flour
½ cup (100g) white long-grain rice
½ cup firmly packed fresh coriander leaves
2 tablespoons lemon juice

1 Place chickpeas in medium bowl, cover with water, stand overnight; drain. Rinse under cold water; drain.

2 Melt butter in large saucepan; cook onion, celery and garlic, stirring, until onion softens. Add ginger, cinnamon, pepper and saffron; cook, stirring, until fragrant. Add lamb; cook, stirring, about 5 minutes or until lamb is browned. Add chickpeas and tomato; cook, stirring, about 5 minutes or until tomato softens.

3 Stir the water into soup mixture; bring to a boil. Reduce heat; simmer, covered, 45 minutes. Add lentils; simmer, covered, 1 hour.

4 Blend flour with ½ cup of slightly cooled broth in a small bowl; return to pan with rice. Cook, stirring, until soup comes to a boil and thickens slightly. Remove from heat; stir in coriander and juice.

• **preparation time** 25 minutes (plus standing time) **cooking time** 2 hours 15 minutes **serves** 8 **per serving** 8.6g total fat (4g saturated fat); 1095kJ (262 cal); 23.6g carbohydrate; 20.1g protein; 4.8g fibre

It's a good idea to serve this soup in large shallow bowls, so that the pork stands up out of the soup, allowing the crackling to remain crisp.

asian broth with crisp pork belly

½ cup (100g) dried soy beans
1kg boned pork belly, rind-on
1½ teaspoons cooking salt
1 teaspoon five-spice powder
2 cups (500ml) water
1 litre (4 cups) chicken stock
1 fresh small red thai chilli, chopped finely
2 star anise
5cm piece fresh ginger (25g), slivered
⅓ cup (80ml) hoisin sauce
500g choy sum, sliced thinly
3 green onions, sliced thinly

Since the beans have to be soaked overnight in any case, the pork benefits from being prepared the day before and refrigerated overnight. This helps the rind dry out, which, in turn, ensures a crisp crackling at the end of cooking. We suggest you make your own stock for this recipe; see the recipe on page 112.

1 Place beans in small bowl, cover with cold water; stand overnight.
2 Place pork on board, rind-side up; using sharp knife, score pork by making shallow cuts diagonally in both directions at 1cm intervals. Rub combined salt and half the five-spice into cuts; slice pork into 10 pieces. Place pork, rind-side up, on tray, cover loosely; refrigerate overnight.
3 Preheat oven to 240°C/220°C fan-forced.
4 Rinse beans under cold water; drain. Place beans in medium saucepan of boiling water; return to a boil. Reduce heat; simmer, uncovered, until tender. Drain.
5 Meanwhile, place pork on metal rack set over shallow baking dish; roast, uncovered, 30 minutes. Reduce oven temperature to 160°C/140°C fan-forced; roast pork, uncovered, about 45 minutes or until crackling is browned and crisp. Cut pork pieces in half.
6 Place beans in large saucepan with the water, stock, chilli, star anise, ginger, sauce and remaining five-spice; bring to a boil. Reduce heat; simmer, covered, 30 minutes. Stir in choy sum and onion.
7 Serve bowls of soup topped with pork.
• **preparation time** 20 minutes (plus standing and refrigeration time)
cooking time 2 hours **serves** 4
per serving 59.6g total fat (20.2g saturated fat); 3687kJ (882 cal); 12.4g carbohydrate; 72.2g protein; 6.2g fibre

minestrone

2 ham hocks (1kg)
1 medium brown onion (150g), quartered
1 trimmed celery stalk (100g), chopped coarsely
1 teaspoon black peppercorns
1 bay leaf
4 litres (16 cups) water
1 tablespoon olive oil
2 trimmed celery stalks (200g), chopped finely
1 large carrot (180g), chopped finely
3 cloves garlic, crushed
¼ cup (70g) tomato paste
2 large tomatoes (440g), chopped finely
1 small leek (200g), sliced thinly
1 cup (100g) small pasta shells
420g can white beans, rinsed, drained
½ cup coarsely chopped fresh flat-leaf parsley
½ cup coarsely chopped fresh basil
½ cup (40g) shaved parmesan cheese

You can make the broth either the day before or in the morning of the day you want to finish preparing the minestrone so that it chills long enough for the fat to solidify on top; skim it away before reheating the broth.

1 Preheat oven to 220°C/200°C fan-forced.
2 Roast hocks and onion in baking dish, uncovered, 30 minutes. Combine with coarsely chopped celery, peppercorns, bay leaf and the water in large saucepan; bring to a boil. Simmer, uncovered, 2 hours.
3 Remove hocks from soup. Strain broth through muslin-lined sieve or colander into large heatproof bowl; discard solids. Allow broth to cool, cover; refrigerate until cold. When cool, remove ham from bones; shred coarsely. Discard bones.
4 Meanwhile, heat oil in large saucepan; cook finely chopped celery and carrot, stirring, 2 minutes. Add ham, garlic, paste and tomato; cook, stirring, 2 minutes.
5 Discard fat from surface of broth. Place broth in measuring jug; add enough water to make 2 litres. Add broth to pan; bring to a boil. Simmer, covered, 20 minutes.
6 Add leek, pasta and beans; bring to a boil. Simmer, uncovered, until pasta is just tender. Remove from heat; stir in herbs. Serve soup sprinkled with cheese.

• **preparation time** 40 minutes (plus refrigeration time)
cooking time 3 hours 35 minutes **serves** 6
per serving 7.2g total fat (2.4g saturated fat); 865kJ (207 cal); 19.6g carbohydrate; 12.7g protein; 6.1g fibre

Traditionally, black bean soup is served with small bowls of various complementary condiments such as chopped hard-boiled egg, sour cream, paper-thin slices of red onion, wedges of lime, and chopped chilli and coriander leaves. Diners help themselves to whatever flavours they want to stir into their individual bowls of soup.

cuban black bean

2½ cups (500g) dried black beans
1kg ham bone
¼ cup (60ml) olive oil
2 medium brown onions (300g), chopped finely
1 medium red capsicum (200g), chopped finely
4 cloves garlic, crushed
1 tablespoon ground cumin
1 teaspoon dried chilli flakes
400g can chopped tomatoes
2.5 litres (10 cups) water
1 tablespoon dried oregano
2 teaspoons ground black pepper
¼ cup (60ml) lime juice
2 medium tomatoes (300g), chopped finely
¼ cup coarsely chopped fresh coriander
2 limes, quartered

Some Cuban chefs like to mash half the beans then return them to the soup, giving it a smooth, almost velvet-like consistency.

1 Place beans in medium bowl, cover with water, stand overnight; drain. Rinse under cold water; drain.
2 Preheat oven to 220°C/200°C fan-forced.
3 Roast ham bone on oven tray, uncovered, 30 minutes.
4 Meanwhile, heat oil in large saucepan; cook onion, capsicum and garlic, stirring, until vegetables soften. Add cumin and chilli; cook, stirring, 1 minute. Add beans and ham bone to pan with undrained canned tomatoes, the water, oregano and pepper; bring to a boil. Reduce heat; simmer, uncovered, 1½ hours.
5 Remove ham bone from soup. When cool enough to handle, remove ham from bone, shred coarsely. Discard bone.
6 Return ham to soup; bring to a boil. Reduce heat, simmer, uncovered, until soup is hot. Remove from heat; stir in juice, fresh tomato and coriander.
7 Serve bowls of soup with lime wedges.
• **preparation time** 30 minutes (plus standing time) **cooking time** 2 hours 15 minutes **serves** 8 **per serving** 9.4g total fat (1.6g saturated fat); 1279kJ (306 cal); 29.2g carbohydrate; 20.4g protein; 10.9g fibre

Use crisp, crunchy fresh water chestnuts for this recipe if they are in season; frozen fresh water chestnuts also can be found in many Asian grocers. You need to buy about 5 medium-sized ones for this soup.

pork and vegetable wonton

3 litres (12 cups) water
1kg chicken bones
1 small brown onion (80g), quartered
1 medium carrot (120g), quartered
4cm piece fresh ginger (20g), grated
2 fresh small red thai chillies, halved lengthways
150g pork mince
1 clove garlic, crushed
1 green onion, chopped finely
2 tablespoons finely chopped water chestnuts
2 tablespoons finely chopped fresh coriander
1 teaspoon sesame oil
2 tablespoons chinese cooking wine
¼ cup (60ml) light soy sauce
2 teaspoons white sugar
12 wonton wrappers
1 cup firmly packed watercress sprigs
4 fresh shiitake mushrooms, sliced thinly

Uncooked wontons can be frozen until required; cook, straight from the freezer, in the broth.

1   Place the water in large saucepan with bones, brown onion, carrot, three-quarters of the ginger and 2 chilli halves; bring to a boil. Reduce heat; simmer, covered, 2 hours.
2   Strain broth through muslin-lined sieve or colander into large heatproof bowl; discard solids. Allow broth to cool; cover, refrigerate.
3   Meanwhile, chop remaining chilli finely; combine in bowl with remaining ginger, pork, garlic, green onion, water chestnut, coriander, oil, 2 teaspoons of the wine and 1 teaspoon each of the sauce and the sugar.
4   Place 1 level tablespoon of filling in centre of each wonton wrapper; brush edges with a little water. Gather edges around filling; pinch together.
5   Skim and discard fat from surface of broth. Return broth to large saucepan with remaining wine, sauce and sugar; bring to a boil. Add wontons, reduce heat; cook, uncovered, about 5 minutes or until wontons are cooked.
6   Divide watercress, mushrooms and wontons among bowls; ladle broth into bowls.
•   **preparation time** 40 minutes **cooking time** 2 hours 10 minutes **serves** 4
    per serving 5.3g total fat (1.6g saturated fat); 853kJ (204 cal); 20.5g carbohydrate; 14.6g protein; 2.4g fibre

Vegetable

curried cauliflower

1 tablespoon olive oil
1 medium brown onion (150g), chopped finely
2 cloves garlic, crushed
½ cup (150g) mild curry paste
2 litres (8 cups) water
1 small cauliflower (1kg), trimmed, chopped coarsely
2 medium potatoes (400g), chopped coarsely
1 tablespoon tomato paste
1 cup (250ml) buttermilk
½ cup loosely packed fresh coriander leaves

1   Heat oil in large saucepan; cook onion and garlic, stirring, until onion softens. Add curry paste; cook, stirring, 5 minutes.
2   Add the water, cauliflower, potato and paste; bring to a boil. Reduce heat; simmer, uncovered, about 15 minutes or until vegetables are tender. Cool 15 minutes.
3   Blend or process soup, in batches, until smooth. Return soup to same cleaned pan, add buttermilk; stir over low heat until hot.
4   Serve bowls of soup sprinkled with coriander and, if desired, accompanied with warmed naan bread.
•   **preparation time** 20 minutes (plus cooling time) **cooking time** 25 minutes **serves** 6 **per serving** 12.1g total fat (1.8g saturated fat); 936kJ (224 cal); 16.8g carbohydrate; 8.3g protein; 6.8g fibre

roasted capsicum with fried provolone polenta

4 medium red capsicums (800g)
2 cloves garlic, unpeeled
1 tablespoon olive oil
1 medium brown onion (150g), chopped finely
1 teaspoon sweet paprika
3 cups (750ml) water
1 litre (4 cups) chicken stock
½ cup (125ml) cream
2 teaspoons white sugar
1 tablespoon finely chopped fresh chives

We suggest you make your own stock for this recipe; see the recipe on page 112.

1   Three hours before, make provolone polenta.

2   Quarter capsicums, discard seeds and membranes. Roast capsicum and garlic under grill or in very hot oven, skin-side up, until skin blisters and blackens. Cover capsicum pieces in plastic or paper for 5 minutes, peel away skin. Peel garlic; chop coarsely.

3   Heat oil in large saucepan; cook onion, stirring, until softened. Add paprika; cook, stirring, until fragrant.

4   Add the water, stock, capsicum and garlic; bring to a boil. Reduce heat; simmer, uncovered, 40 minutes. Cool 15 minutes.

5   Meanwhile, turn polenta onto board, trim edges; cut in half lengthways, cut each half into 9 finger-sized slices. Cook polenta, in batches, in heated oiled large frying pan until browned both sides.

6   Blend or process soup, in batches, until smooth. Return soup to same cleaned pan, add cream and sugar; stir over medium heat until hot.

7   Serve bowls of soup sprinkled with chives, accompanied with fried polenta.

•   preparation time 15 minutes (plus refrigeration time) cooking time 1 hour 15 minutes serves 6 per serving 12.7g total fat (6.5g saturated fat); 727kJ (174 cal); 9.9g carbohydrate; 4.1g protein; 2.6g fibre

accompaniment

provolone polenta
Lightly oil 20cm x 30cm lamington pan; line base and two long sides with baking paper, extending paper 5cm over long sides. Bring 3½ cups of water to a boil in medium saucepan. Gradually add 1 cup polenta, stirring constantly. Reduce heat; simmer, stirring, about 10 minutes or until polenta thickens. Stir in 20g butter and 1 cup coarsely grated provolone cheese. Spread polenta into pan, cover; refrigerate about 3 hours or until firm.
serves 6 per serving 8.9g total fat (5.5g saturated fat); 757kJ (181 cal); 17.3g carbohydrate; 7.6g protein; 0.7g fibre

potato and leek

2 medium potatoes (400g), chopped coarsely
2 medium carrots (240g), chopped coarsely
1 large brown onion (200g), chopped coarsely
1 medium tomato (150g), chopped coarsely
1 trimmed celery stalk (100g), chopped coarsely
1.5 litres (6 cups) water
1 tablespoon olive oil
50g butter
4 medium potatoes (800g), chopped coarsely, extra
1 large leek (500g), sliced thickly
300ml cream
2 tablespoons finely chopped fresh chives
1 tablespoon finely chopped fresh basil
1 tablespoon finely chopped fresh dill

1 Combine potato, carrot, onion, tomato, celery and the water in large saucepan; bring to a boil. Reduce heat; simmer, uncovered, 20 minutes. Strain broth through muslin-lined sieve or colander into large heatproof bowl; discard solids.
2 Heat oil and butter in same cleaned pan; cook extra potato and leek, covered, 15 minutes, stirring occasionally. Add broth; bring to a boil. Reduce heat; simmer, covered, 15 minutes. Cool 15 minutes.
3 Meanwhile, make croûtons.
4 Blend or process soup, in batches, until smooth. Return soup to same cleaned pan, add cream; stir over medium heat until hot.
5 Serve bowls of soup sprinkled with combined herbs then topped with croûtons.
• **preparation time** 30 minutes (plus cooling time) **cooking time** 55 minutes **serves** 4
per serving 47.9g total fat (28.8g saturated fat); 2822kJ (675 cal); 46.3g carbohydrate; 11g protein; 9.8g fibre

accompaniment

croûtons
Cut and discard crusts from 2 slices wholemeal bread; cut bread into 1cm pieces. Melt 50g butter in medium frying pan. Add bread; cook, stirring, until croûtons are browned lightly. Drain on absorbent paper.
serves 4 **per serving** 10.7g total fat (6.8g saturated fat); 535kJ (128 cal); 6.2g carbohydrate; 1.6g protein; 1g fibre

spring vegetable broth
with cheese-filled zucchini flowers

2.5 litres (10 cups) water
3 medium pontiac potatoes (600g), unpeeled, halved
2 medium tomatoes (300g), quartered
2 medium carrots (240g), chopped coarsely
2 trimmed celery stalks (200g), chopped coarsely
1 large brown onion (200g), chopped coarsely
100g mushrooms, halved
2 cloves garlic, unpeeled, bruised
8 black peppercorns
1 bay leaf
2 sprigs fresh flat-leaf parsley
2 sprigs fresh dill
12 baby zucchini with flowers attached (240g)
170g asparagus, trimmed, chopped coarsely
150g sugar snap peas, halved diagonally

1   Place the water in large saucepan with potato, tomato, carrot, celery, onion, mushrooms, garlic, peppercorns, bay leaf, parsley and dill; bring to a boil. Reduce heat; simmer, uncovered, 1½ hours. Strain broth through muslin-lined sieve or colander into large heatproof bowl. Discard solids.

2   Meanwhile, separate flowers from each zucchini. (Save flowers for cheese-filled zucchini flowers; see accompaniment, below.) Chop zucchini coarsely; reserve for broth.

3   Make cheese-filled zucchini flowers.

4   Return broth to same cleaned pan; bring to a boil. Remove from heat; add reserved zucchini, asparagus and peas.

5   Serve bowls of soup topped with zucchini flowers.

•   preparation time 25 minutes cooking time 1 hour 40 minutes serves 4
per serving 0.8g total fat (0g saturated fat); 790kJ (189 cal);
30.4g carbohydrate; 9.6g protein; 10.4g fibre

accompaniment

cheese-filled zucchini flowers
Combine 150g soft goat cheese, 1 teaspoon finely grated lemon rind, 1 tablespoon lemon juice and 1 tablespoon finely chopped fresh dill in small bowl. Discard stamens from zucchini flowers; fill flowers with cheese mixture, twist petal tops to enclose filling.
serves 4 per serving 5.9g total fat (3.9g saturated fat); 314kJ (75 cal);
0.5g carbohydrate; 5g protein; 0.1g fibre

chilled yogurt, cucumber and mint

3 medium green cucumbers (510g), peeled, grated coarsely
1 clove garlic, quartered
1 tablespoon lemon juice
1 tablespoon coarsely chopped fresh mint
500g greek-style yogurt

1 Place cucumber in sieve over bowl, cover; refrigerate 3 hours or overnight. Reserve cucumber liquid in bowl. Squeeze excess liquid from cucumber.

2 Blend or process cucumber, garlic, juice and mint until mixture is smooth; transfer to large bowl. Stir yogurt into cucumber mixture then add reserved cucumber liquid, a little at a time, stirring, until soup is of desired consistency.

3 Serve bowls of soup topped with extra mint and toasted turkish bread, if desired.

• **preparation time** 10 minutes (plus refrigeration time) **serves** 4
per serving 8.9g total fat (5.7g saturated fat); 715kJ (171 cal); 13.9g carbohydrate; 7.6g protein; 0.8g fibre

green pea with mint pistou

1 tablespoon olive oil
1 small leek (200g), sliced thinly
1 clove garlic, crushed
2 large potatoes (600g), chopped coarsely
3 cups (360g) frozen peas
3 cups (750ml) water
2 cups (500ml) vegetable stock
mint pistou
2 cups loosely packed fresh mint leaves
¼ cup (20g) finely grated parmesan cheese
1 tablespoon lemon juice
1 clove garlic, quartered
¼ cup (60ml) olive oil

We suggest you make your own stock for this recipe; see the recipe on page 113.

1 Heat oil in large saucepan; cook leek and garlic, stirring, until leek softens. Add potato, peas, the water and stock; bring to a boil. Reduce heat; simmer, covered, about 10 minutes or until potato is tender. Cool 15 minutes.
2 Meanwhile, make mint pistou.
3 Blend or process soup, in batches, until smooth. Return soup to same cleaned pan; stir over medium heat until hot.
4 Serve bowls of soup topped with pistou.
mint pistou Blend or process ingredients until smooth.

● **preparation time** 10 minutes (plus cooling time) **cooking time** 20 minutes **serves** 4
per serving 20.9g total fat (3.7g saturated fat); 1634kJ (391 cal); 32.2g carbohydrate; 12.9g protein; 12g fibre

pumpkin and eggplant laksa

700g piece butternut pumpkin, diced into 2cm pieces
5 baby eggplants (300g), sliced thickly
3 cups (750ml) vegetable stock
1⅔ cups (400ml) coconut milk
250g rice stick noodles
500g buk choy, chopped coarsely
2 tablespoons lime juice
1¼ cups (100g) bean sprouts
6 green onions, sliced thinly
½ cup loosely packed fresh coriander leaves
½ cup loosely packed vietnamese mint leaves
laksa paste
7 medium dried red chillies
½ cup (125ml) boiling water
1 tablespoon peanut oil
3 cloves garlic, quartered
1 medium brown onion (150g), chopped coarsely
10cm stick fresh lemon grass (20g), trimmed, chopped finely
4cm piece fresh ginger (20g), grated
1 tablespoon halved macadamias
roots from 1 bunch coriander, washed, chopped coarsely
1 teaspoon ground turmeric
1 teaspoon ground coriander
2 teaspoons salt
¼ cup loosely packed vietnamese mint leaves

Keep the roots from the bunch of fresh coriander you buy for this recipe because they are used, washed and chopped, in the laksa paste.

1 Make laksa paste.
2 Place ½ cup of the paste in large saucepan; cook, stirring, until fragrant. Add pumpkin and eggplant; cook, stirring, 2 minutes. Add stock and coconut milk; bring to a boil. Reduce heat; simmer, covered, about 10 minutes or until vegetables are just tender.
3 Meanwhile, place noodles in large heatproof bowl, cover with boiling water, stand until just tender; drain.
4 Stir buk choy into laksa; return to a boil. Remove from heat; stir in juice.
5 Divide noodles among serving bowls; ladle laksa over noodles, sprinkle with combined sprouts, onion and herbs.
    laksa paste Cover chillies with the water in small heatproof bowl, stand 10 minutes; drain. Blend or process chillies with remaining ingredients until mixture forms a smooth paste. Measure ½ cup of the paste for this recipe; freeze the remainder, covered, for future use.

• preparation time 45 minutes cooking time 20 minutes serves 6
   per serving 20.7g total fat (13.3g saturated fat); 1405kJ; (336 cal); 25.8g carbohydrate; 7.9g protein; 8.4g fibre

cream of roasted fennel with capsicum aïoli

2 medium fennel bulbs (600g)
1 large brown onion (200g), chopped coarsely
4 cloves garlic, unpeeled, bruised
2 teaspoons dried fennel seeds
1 tablespoon olive oil
2 cups (500ml) vegetable stock
1 cup (250ml) milk
1 cup (250ml) water
2 teaspoons lemon juice
capsicum aïoli
1 medium red capsicum (200g)
2 cloves garlic
1 egg yolk
1 tablespoon lemon juice
½ teaspoon dijon mustard
⅓ cup (80ml) olive oil

We suggest you make your own stock for this recipe; see the recipe on page 113.

1   Preheat oven to 200°C/180°C fan-forced.
2   Trim fennel; reserve 4 frond tips. Chop fennel coarsely; combine with onion, garlic, seeds and oil in shallow medium baking dish. Roast, uncovered, 30 minutes; cover, roast about 20 minutes or until tender.
3   When cool enough to handle, squeeze garlic into large saucepan; discard skins. Add roasted fennel mixture to pan with stock, milk and the water; bring to a boil. Reduce heat; simmer, uncovered, 10 minutes. Cool 15 minutes.
4   Meanwhile, make capsicum aïoli.
5   Blend or process soup, in batches, until smooth. Return soup to same cleaned pan, add juice; stir over medium heat until hot.
6   Serve bowls of soup drizzled with aïoli then topped with reserved fronds.
    capsicum aïoli Quarter capsicum; discard seeds and membrane. Roast under grill or in hot oven, skin-side up, until skin blisters and blackens. Cover capsicum in plastic or paper for 5 minutes; peel away skin then chop capsicum coarsely. Blend or process garlic, yolk, juice and mustard until mixture is smooth. With motor operating, add oil in a thin, steady stream; process until aïoli thickens. Add capsicum; process until smooth. (Can be made a day ahead; cover and refrigerate overnight.)
•   **preparation time** 10 minutes (plus cooling time) **cooking time** 1 hour 10 minutes **serves** 4 **per serving** 27g total fat (5.3g saturated fat); 1367kJ (327 cal); 13g carbohydrate; 5.6g protein; 6g fibre

cream of kumara with rosemary sourdough

1 tablespoon olive oil
2 medium kumara (800g), chopped coarsely
1 medium brown onion (150g), chopped coarsely
2 cloves garlic, quartered
2 teaspoons coarsely chopped fresh rosemary
1 teaspoon finely grated lemon rind
2 cups (500ml) vegetable stock
2 cups (500ml) water
1 tablespoon lemon juice
½ cup (125ml) cream

1 Heat oil in large frying pan; cook kumara, onion and garlic, stirring, 10 minutes. Add rosemary, rind, stock and the water; bring to a boil. Reduce heat; simmer, covered, about 15 minutes or until kumara is soft. Cool 15 minutes.
2 Meanwhile, make rosemary sourdough.
3 Blend or process soup, in batches, until smooth. Return soup to same cleaned pan, add juice; stir over medium heat until hot.
4 Serve bowls of soup drizzled with cream, accompanied with sourdough.
• **preparation time** 10 minutes (plus cooling time) **cooking time** 30 minutes **serves** 6
per serving 12.3g total fat (6.4g saturated fat); 890kJ (213 cal);
20.4g carbohydrate; 3.5g protein; 3.6g fibre

accompaniment

rosemary sourdough
Preheat oven to 180°C/160°C fan-forced. Slice 1 loaf sourdough bread into 3cm pieces. Combine 2 tablespoons olive oil and 2 teaspoons finely chopped fresh rosemary in large bowl; add bread, turn to coat in mixture. Place bread on oven tray; toast bread, both sides, about 15 minutes.
serves 6 **per serving** 13.5g total fat (2g saturated fat); 2092kJ (500 cal);
75.8g carbohydrate; 14.5g protein; 7.8g fibre

jerusalem artichoke with caramelised onion and artichoke crisps

1 tablespoon lemon juice
1 litre (4 cups) water
10 medium jerusalem artichokes (600g)
1 tablespoon olive oil
1 large brown onion (200g), chopped coarsely
4 cloves garlic, crushed
2 medium potatoes (400g), chopped coarsely
1 litre (4 cups) chicken stock
caramelised onion
25g butter
2 large brown onions (400g), sliced thinly
2 teaspoons brown sugar
1 tablespoon balsamic vinegar
artichoke crisps
4 medium jerusalem artichokes (240g), unpeeled, sliced thinly
1 tablespoon olive oil
½ teaspoon salt
¼ teaspoon ground black pepper

Acidulated water is cold water into which white vinegar or lemon juice or pulp has been added, at about a proportion of 1 tablespoon per litre of water, to prevent the cut surfaces of foods, such as apples or artichokes, from discolouring. We suggest you make your own stock for this recipe; see the recipe on page 112.

1   Combine juice and the water in large bowl. Peel and coarsely chop artichokes; place in acidulated water.
2   Heat oil in large saucepan; cook onion and garlic, stirring, until onion softens. Add drained artichokes, potato and stock; bring to a boil. Reduce heat; simmer, covered, about 20 minutes or until potato is tender. Cool 15 minutes.
3   Meanwhile, make caramelised onion. Make artichoke crisps.
4   Blend or process soup, in batches, until smooth. Reheat soup in same pan.
5   Serve bowls of soup topped with onion then crisps.

caramelised onion Melt butter in medium saucepan; cook onion over medium heat, stirring, about 10 minutes or until soft. Add sugar and vinegar; cook, stirring, about 10 minutes or until caramelised.

artichoke crisps Preheat oven to 200°C/180°C fan-forced. Combine ingredients in medium bowl; place artichoke, in single layer, on wire rack set over baking dish. Roast, uncovered, about 20 minutes or until crisp.

●   preparation time 40 minutes (plus cooling time) **cooking time** 40 minutes **serves** 4 **per serving** 15.4g total fat (4.9g saturated fat); 1329kJ (318 cal); 29.7g carbohydrate; 10.4g protein; 10.1g fibre

spicy tomato with ricotta ravioli and rocket pesto

⅓ cup (80g) ricotta cheese
2 tablespoons finely grated parmesan cheese
2 fresh lasagne sheets (100g)
1 egg, beaten lightly
1 tablespoon olive oil
1 large brown onion (200g), chopped coarsely
1 clove garlic, crushed
1 fresh small red thai chilli, chopped finely
700g egg tomatoes, seeded, chopped coarsely
2 trimmed celery stalks (200g), chopped coarsely
2 cups (500ml) vegetable stock
410g can tomato puree
rocket pesto
20g baby rocket leaves
¼ cup (35g) roasted unsalted pistachios
¼ cup (20g) coarsely grated parmesan cheese
1 clove garlic, quartered
2 tablespoons olive oil
1 tablespoon lemon juice
1 tablespoon water

1 Combine cheeses in small bowl. Cut each lasagne sheet into 24 squares. Place level half-teaspoons of cheese mixture in centre of 24 squares, brush around edges with egg; top each with remaining squares, press around edges firmly to seal. Place ravioli, in single layer, on tray, cover; refrigerate 20 minutes.

2 Meanwhile, heat oil in large saucepan; cook onion, garlic and chilli, stirring, until onion softens. Add chopped tomato, celery and stock; bring to a boil. Reduce heat; simmer, covered, about 20 minutes or until celery is tender. Cool 15 minutes.

3 Make rocket pesto.

4 Blend or process soup, in batches, until smooth. Return soup to same cleaned pan, add tomato puree; bring to a boil. Reduce heat; simmer, uncovered, 10 minutes.

5 Meanwhile, cook ravioli, uncovered, in large saucepan of boiling salted water until they float to the surface; drain then stir into soup.

6 Serve bowls of soup, with ravioli, topped with pesto.

rocket pesto Blend or process rocket, nuts, cheese and garlic until chopped coarsely. With motor operating, gradually add oil; process until mixture forms a thick paste. Stir in juice and water.

• preparation time 40 minutes (plus refrigeration and cooling time)
cooking time 40 minutes serves 4
per serving 25.1g total fat (6.1g saturated fat); 1814kJ (434 cal); 32.6g carbohydrate; 15.8g protein; 8.2g fibre

cream of spinach with lemon fetta toasts

40g butter
1 large brown onion (200g), chopped finely
2 cloves garlic, crushed
3 medium potatoes (600g), chopped coarsely
3 cups (750ml) chicken stock
1 litre (4 cups) water
250g trimmed spinach, chopped coarsely
¾ cup (180ml) cream

We suggest you make your own stock for this recipe; see the recipe on page 112. You need 1kg of untrimmed spinach to get the amount of trimmed spinach needed for this recipe.

1 Melt butter in large saucepan; cook onion and garlic, stirring, until onion softens. Add potato, stock and the water; bring to a boil. Reduce heat; simmer, covered, about 15 minutes or until potato is tender. Stir in spinach; cool 15 minutes.
2 Meanwhile, make lemon fetta toasts.
3 Blend or process soup, in batches, until smooth. Return soup to same cleaned pan, add cream; stir over medium heat until hot.
4 Serve bowls of soup with toasts.

• **preparation time** 20 minutes (plus cooling time) **cooking time** 35 minutes **serves** 6
per serving 19g total fat (12.3g saturated fat); 1078kJ (258 cal); 15.3g carbohydrate; 5.1g protein; 3.6g fibre

accompaniment

lemon fetta toasts
Preheat grill. Combine 150g fetta cheese with 1 teaspoon finely grated lemon rind. Cut 1 small french bread stick into 1.5cm slices; discard end pieces. Toast slices one side; turn, sprinkle each slice with fetta mixture and another 1 teaspoon finely grated lemon rind. Grill toasts until browned lightly.
serves 6 **per serving** 6.6g total fat (3.9g saturated fat); 548kJ (131 cal); 11.1g carbohydrate; 6.3g protein; 0.8g fibre

We used a teriyaki-flavoured tofu in this recipe, available already marinated in soy sauce and rice wine. Various-flavoured marinated tofu pieces can be found, cryovac-packed, in the refrigerated section in most supermarkets and Asian food stores. Good for general use, yellow miso, often sold called "shinshu", is a deep-yellow, smooth fermented soya bean paste, which is fairly salty and tart.

tofu and spinach miso

1.5 litres (6 cups) water
¼ cup (75g) yellow miso
1 tablespoon japanese soy sauce
3cm piece fresh ginger (15g), grated
100g dried soba noodles
200g marinated tofu, cut into 2cm pieces
4 green onions, sliced thinly
100g baby spinach leaves
1 fresh long red chilli, sliced thinly

1 Place the water in large saucepan with miso, sauce and ginger; bring to a boil. Add noodles, return to a boil; cook, uncovered, about 3 minutes or until noodles are just tender.

2 Remove from heat, add tofu, onion and spinach to broth; stir gently until spinach just wilts.

3 Serve bowls of soup sprinkled with chilli.

• preparation time 10 minutes cooking time 10 minutes serves 4
per serving 4.9g total fat (0.7g saturated fat); 803kJ (192 cal); 22.9g carbohydrate; 12.1g protein; 3.8g fibre

beetroot cream with chive and goat cheese dumplings

30g butter
1 tablespoon olive oil
1 large brown onion (200g), chopped coarsely
2 cloves garlic, crushed
1 teaspoon sweet paprika
½ cup (125ml) dry white wine
5 medium beetroots (1.5kg), trimmed, peeled, chopped coarsely
1 litre (4 cups) chicken stock
¾ cup (180ml) cream
2 tablespoons coarsely chopped fresh chives

We suggest you make your own stock for this recipe; see the recipe on page 112.

1 Heat butter and oil in large saucepan; cook onion and garlic, stirring, until onion is tender. Add paprika; cook, stirring, until fragrant. Add wine; simmer, uncovered, about 2 minutes or until reduced by half. Add beetroot and stock; bring to a boil. Reduce heat; simmer, uncovered, stirring occasionally, about 40 minutes or until beetroot softens. Cool 15 minutes.

2 Meanwhile, make chive and goat cheese dumplings.

3 Blend or process soup, in batches, until smooth. Return soup to same cleaned pan, add cream; stir over medium heat until hot.

4 Serve bowls of soup topped with dumplings and chives.

• preparation time 25 minutes (plus cooling time) cooking time 50 minutes serves 4
per serving 31.6g total fat (18.1g saturated fat); 2090kJ (500 cal); 33.5g carbohydrate; 10.8g protein; 11.1g fibre

accompaniment

chive and goat cheese dumplings
Combine 110g crumbled goat cheese, 2 egg yolks, ⅓ cup self-raising flour, ⅓ cup finely grated parmesan cheese and 1 tablespoon finely chopped fresh chives in small bowl. Drop level tablespoons of mixture into large saucepan of simmering water; cook, uncovered, about 5 minutes or until dumplings are cooked through. Remove using slotted spoon; drain on absorbent paper.
serves 4 per serving 9.6g total fat (5.2g saturated fat); 652kJ (156 cal); 8.5g carbohydrate; 9g protein; 0.5g fibre

french onion with gruyère croûtons

50g butter
4 large brown onions (800g), halved, sliced thinly
¾ cup (180ml) dry white wine
3 cups (750ml) water
1 litre (4 cups) beef stock
1 bay leaf
1 tablespoon plain flour
1 teaspoon fresh thyme leaves

We suggest you make your own stock for this recipe; see the recipe on page 112.

1 Melt butter in large saucepan; cook onion, stirring, about 30 minutes or until caramelised.

2 Meanwhile, bring wine to a boil in large saucepan; boil 1 minute. Stir in the water, stock and bay leaf; return to a boil. Remove from heat.

3 Stir flour into onion mixture; cook, stirring, 2 minutes. Gradually add hot broth mixture, stirring, until mixture boils and thickens slightly. Reduce heat; simmer, uncovered, stirring occasionally, 20 minutes. Discard bay leaf; stir in thyme.

4 Meanwhile, make gruyère croûtons.

5 Serve bowls of soup topped with croûtons.

• preparation time 30 minutes cooking time 50 minutes serves 4
per serving 1.1g fat (0.7g saturated fat); 96kJ (23 cal); 1.4g carbohydrate; 1g protein; 0.3g fibre

accompaniment

gruyère croûtons
Preheat grill. Finely grate 60g gruyère cheese. Cut 1 small french bread stick into 1.5cm slices; discard end pieces. Toast slices one side then turn and sprinkle equal amounts of cheese over untoasted sides; grill croûtons until cheese browns lightly.
serves 4 per serving 5.7g total fat (3g saturated fat); 623kJ (149 cal); 16.6g carbohydrate; 7.1g protein; 1.2g fibre

A chilled soup that originated in the southern province of Andalusia in Spain, where the long, sunny summers produce an explosion of vegetables, gazpacho has a wonderfully refreshing flavour and is even better if made ahead, so the individual flavours can shine through. Refrigerate it, covered, overnight to taste it at its best.

gazpacho

3 cups (750ml) tomato juice
8 medium egg tomatoes (600g), chopped coarsely
1 medium red onion (170g), chopped coarsely
1 clove garlic, quartered
1 lebanese cucumber (130g), chopped coarsely
1 small red capsicum (150g), chopped coarsely
2 teaspoons Tabasco
4 green onions, chopped finely
½ lebanese cucumber (65g), seeded, chopped finely
½ small yellow capsicum (75g), chopped finely
2 teaspoons olive oil
1 tablespoon vodka
2 tablespoons finely chopped fresh coriander

1 Blend or process juice, tomato, red onion, garlic, coarsely chopped cucumber and red capsicum, in batches, until pureed. Strain through sieve into large bowl, cover; refrigerate 3 hours.
2 Combine remaining ingredients in small bowl.
3 Serves bowls of soup topped with vegetable mixture.
• preparation time 25 minutes (plus refrigeration time) serves 4
per serving 2.6g total fat (0.3g saturated fat); 560kJ (134 cal); 17.7g carbohydrate; 4.7g protein; 5.2g fibre

Soup mix is a packaged blend of various dried pulses and grains, among them, lentils, split peas and barley. It is available from supermarkets.

spiced coriander, lentil and barley

1 tablespoon coriander seeds
1 tablespoon cumin seeds
1 tablespoon ghee
6 cloves garlic, crushed
2 fresh small red thai chillies, chopped finely
1¼ cups (250g) soup mix
1 litre (4 cups) chicken stock
3½ cups (875ml) water
1 cup coarsely chopped fresh coriander
⅓ cup (95g) greek-style yogurt
1 tablespoon mango chutney

1 Dry-fry seeds in large saucepan, stirring, until fragrant. Using pestle and mortar, crush seeds.
2 Melt ghee in same pan; cook crushed seeds, garlic and chilli, stirring, 5 minutes.
3 Add soup mix, stock and the water; bring to a boil. Reduce heat; simmer, covered, stirring occasionally, 1 hour. Cool 15 minutes.
4 Blend or process half the soup, in batches, until smooth. Return pureed soup to pan with unprocessed soup; stir over medium heat until hot. Remove from heat; stir in coriander.
5 Serve bowls of soup topped with yogurt and chutney.
• **preparation time** 10 minutes (plus cooling time) **cooking time** 1 hour 20 minutes **serves** 4 **per serving** 7.9g total fat (4.6g saturated fat); 1350kJ (323 cal); 49.7g carbohydrate; 11.4g protein; 3g fibre

cream of mushroom and pancetta

10g dried porcini mushrooms
1 cup (250ml) boiling water
40g butter
1 medium brown onion (150g), chopped coarsely
1 small leek (200g), sliced thinly
250g button mushrooms, sliced thickly
⅓ cup (80ml) dry white wine
3 cups (750ml) chicken stock
1 large potato (300g), chopped coarsely
300ml cream
2 tablespoons coarsely chopped fresh tarragon
6 slices pancetta (90g)

We suggest you make your own stock for this recipe; see the recipe on page 112.

1   Place porcini in small heatproof bowl, cover with the water; stand 30 minutes. Drain through fine sieve into small bowl; reserve liquid. Chop porcini coarsely.

2   Meanwhile, melt butter in large saucepan; cook onion and leek, stirring, until vegetables soften. Add button mushrooms; cook, stirring, about 10 minutes or until mushrooms soften and liquid evaporates. Add wine; cook, stirring, about 5 minutes or until liquid reduces by half. Add reserved porcini liquid, stock and potato; bring to a boil. Reduce heat; simmer, uncovered, about 10 minutes or until potato is tender. Remove soup from heat; cool 15 minutes.

3   Blend or process soup, in batches, until smooth, return to same cleaned pan; bring to a boil. Add cream; reduce heat, stir over medium heat until soup is hot. Remove from heat; stir in tarragon.

4   Meanwhile, cook pancetta in heated medium frying pan until crisp; drain on absorbent paper.

5   Serve bowls of soup sprinkled with porcini and crumbled pancetta.

•   **preparation time** 30 minutes (plus standing and cooling time)
    cooking time 40 minutes **serves** 4
    per serving 44.9g total fat (28.4g saturated fat); 2228kJ (533 cal); 15.6g carbohydrate; 13g protein; 4g fibre

Packaged

asian beef consommé

Heat a tablespoon of peanut oil until it's really hot in a large saucepan, add 300g beef strips, a chopped red thai chilli and a teaspoon or two of grated fresh ginger; stir-fry until the beef is browned. Pour in a litre of beef consommé or stock; bring to a boil then simmer for about 30 minutes with the lid on. While the beef is cooking, soak 125g bean thread vermicelli for about 5 minutes in a bowl of boiling water, drain then divide among 4 bowls. Add a small bunch of roughly chopped baby buk choy and 2 tablespoons of lime juice to the soup; heat until buk choy wilts then pour soup over the vermicelli.

beef and vegetable with potato dumplings

Boil or microwave a large chopped potato until tender then mash it with an egg yolk, a few teaspoons of chopped chives and 2 tablespoons each of flour and grated cheddar cheese. Shape tablespoons of this mixture into patties and coat them in packaged breadcrumbs. Heat about a ¼ cup of vegetable oil in a frying pan; cook the dumplings until they're browned lightly then drain them well on absorbent paper. Heat two 505g cans of beef and vegetable soup and a cup of water in a pan until it's hot (do not boil). Serve bowls of soup topped with potato dumplings.

each recipe serves 4

thai chicken, pumpkin and coconut

Buy a large barbecued chicken weighing about 900g;
discard the skin and carcass then chop the meat roughly.
Stir ¼ cup red curry paste in a large heated saucepan
until it's fragrant. Add two 420g cans cream of pumpkin
soup, 3¼ cups light coconut milk and 1½ cups chicken
stock to the pan and bring to a boil. Stir in the chicken;
reduce heat to medium then stir until soup is heated through.
Stir in 4 thinly sliced green onions and about a ¼ cup of
roughly chopped basil leaves just before serving.

chinese chicken and corn

You need the same amount of chopped chicken as in
the previous recipe. Heat a teaspoon of vegetable oil
in a large saucepan then cook a teaspoon of freshly
grated ginger and 2 thinly sliced green chillies about
2 minutes. Add two 505g cans chicken and sweet corn
soup, 2½ cups water and 3 cups coarsely chopped
chicken; bring to a boil then simmer. Beat an egg white
in a small jug with a tablespoon of cold water then slowly
pour it into the soup, stirring constantly. Serve soup
sprinkled with sliced green onion.

moroccan vegetable with harissa

Heat 2 teaspoons of olive oil in a large saucepan; stir in
2 crushed garlic cloves until fragrant. Add ¼ cup couscous,
2 tablespoons harissa and 250g fresh halved cherry
tomatoes and stir over medium heat for a minute or two.
Add two 420g cans vegetable soup and 2½ cups water;
bring to a boil then reduce heat and simmer soup, uncovered,
about 5 minutes or until the couscous is just softened. Serve
bowls of soup sprinkled with ¼ cup roasted pine nuts and
a little finely chopped fresh coriander.

italian tomato, bean and basil

Heat 2 teaspoons of olive oil in a small frying pan and
cook a chopped medium onion, 2 crushed garlic cloves
and ⅓ cup fresh basil leaves, stirring, until onion is soft.
Blend this mixture with 420g can condensed tomato soup,
1¾ cups water and 85g chopped roasted red capsicum
until smooth. Combine soup mixture in a saucepan with
425g can rinsed and drained white beans. Bring mixture
to a boil; simmer, uncovered, about 5 minutes. Stir in
⅓ cup cream and serve bowls of soup sprinkled with fresh
baby basil leaves.

potato, bacon and leek with blue cheese toasts
Preheat grill then slice a small french bread stick into
10 even pieces (discard both ends). Toast on one side
then turn and top untoasted side with a mixture of 100g
crumbled blue cheese and 2 thinly sliced green onions;
grill until cheese melts. Chop two rindlesss bacon rashers,
browning them in a medium saucepan before adding
2 finely chopped green onions and 2 cloves crushed
garlic; cook, stirring, until just soft. Add two 505g cans
potato and leek soup, ½ cup milk and ¼ cup water; stir
until hot. Serve soup with toasts.

pumpkin with chilli-crusted pepitas
Preheat oven to 180°C/160°C fan-forced. Combine
½ cup pepitas (dried roasted pumpkin seeds) with about
a teaspoon of dried chilli flakes, 1 teaspoon finely grated
lemon rind and 2 teaspoons of olive oil in small bowl. Place
pepita mixture on an oven tray and roast, uncovered, about
25 minutes or until pepitas are browned lightly. Heat two
505g cans butternut pumpkin soup in a medium saucepan,
stirring; serve bowls of soup sprinkled with pepitas.

Stocks

These recipes can be made up to four days ahead and kept, covered, in the refrigerator. They can also be frozen for up to three months.

beef

2kg meaty beef bones
2 medium brown onions (300g), chopped coarsely
5.5 litres water (22 cups)
2 trimmed celery stalks (200g), chopped coarsely
2 medium carrots (240g), chopped coarsely
3 bay leaves
2 teaspoons black peppercorns
3 litres water (12 cups), extra

1 Preheat oven to 200°C/180°C fan-forced.
2 Roast bones on an oven tray, uncovered, about 1 hour or until browned.
3 Combine bones and onion with the water, celery, carrot, bay leaves and peppercorns in large saucepan or boiler; bring to a boil. Reduce heat; simmer, uncovered, 3 hours, skimming surface occasionally. Add extra water; simmer, uncovered, 1 hour. Strain stock through muslin-lined sieve or colander into large heatproof bowl; discard solids. Allow stock to cool, cover; refrigerate until cold. Skim and discard surface fat before using.
• **preparation time** 10 minutes (plus cooling and refrigeration time) **cooking time** 5 hours **makes** 3.5 litres **per 1 cup (250ml)** 2g total fat (0.9g saturated fat); 259kJ (62 cal); 2.3g carbohydrate; 8g protein; 1.1g fibre

chicken

2kg chicken bones
2 medium onions (300g), chopped coarsely
2 trimmed celery stalks (200g), chopped coarsely
2 medium carrots (240g), chopped coarsely
3 bay leaves
2 teaspoons black peppercorns
5 litres (20 cups) water

1 Combine ingredients in large saucepan or boiler; simmer, uncovered, 2 hours, skimming surface occasionally. Strain stock through muslin-lined sieve or colander into large heatproof bowl; discard solids. Allow stock to cool, cover; refrigerate until cold. Skim and discard surface fat before using.
• **preparation time** 10 minutes (plus cooling and refrigeration time) **cooking time** 2 hours **makes** 3.5 litres **per 1 cup (250ml)** 0.6g total fat (0.2g saturated fat); 105kJ (25 cal); 2.3g carbohydrate; 1.9g protein; 1.1g fibre

fish

1.5kg fish bones
3 litres (12 cups) water
1 medium onion (150g), chopped coarsely
2 trimmed celery stalks (200g), chopped coarsely
2 bay leaves
1 teaspoon black peppercorns

1 Combine ingredients in large saucepan; simmer,
uncovered, 20 minutes. Strain stock through muslin-lined
sieve or colander into large heatproof bowl; discard
solids. Allow stock to cool, cover; refrigerate until cold.
Skim and discard surface fat before using.

● **preparation time** 5 minutes (plus cooling and
refrigeration time) **cooking time** 20 minutes **makes** 2.5 litres
per 1 cup (250ml) 0.2g total fat (0.1g saturated fat); 63kJ
(15 cal); 1.1g carbohydrate; 1.9g protein; 0.6g fibre

vegetable

2 large carrots (360g), chopped coarsely
2 large parsnips (700g), chopped coarsely
4 medium onions (600g), chopped coarsely
10 trimmed celery stalks (1kg), chopped coarsely
4 bay leaves
2 teaspoons black peppercorns
6 litres (24 cups) water

1 Combine ingredients in large saucepan; simmer,
uncovered, 1½ hours. Strain stock through muslin-lined
sieve or colander into large heatproof bowl; discard
solids. Allow stock to cool, cover; refrigerate until cold.
Skim and discard surface fat before using.

● **preparation time** 10 minutes (plus cooling and refrigeration
time) **cooking time** 1 hour 30 minutes **makes** 3.5 litres
per 1 cup (250ml) 0.2g total fat (0g saturated fat); 151kJ
(36 cal); 5.7g carbohydrate; 1.4g protein; 2.9g fibre

Glossary

bacon rashers also known as slices of bacon; made from pork side.

bamboo shoots the tender shoots of bamboo plants, available in cans; drain and rinse before use.

bean sprouts also known as bean shoots; tender new growths of assorted beans and seeds germinated for consumption as sprouts.

beetroot also known as red beets; firm, round root vegetable.

buk choy also known as bak choy, pak choi, chinese white cabbage or chinese chard; has a fresh, mild mustard taste. *Baby buk choy*, also known as pak kat farang or shanghai buk choy, is more tender than buk choy.

buttermilk sold in the refrigerated dairy compartments in supermarkets. Originally the liquid left after cream was separated from milk, today it is commercially made similarly to yogurt.

capsicum also known as bell pepper or pepper; can be red, green, yellow, orange or purplish black. Discard seeds and membranes before use.

cayenne pepper a thin-fleshed, long, extremely hot red chilli; usually purchased dried and ground.

cheese
blue mould-treated cheeses mottled with blue veining.
fetta a crumbly textured goat- or sheep-milk cheese having a sharp, salty taste.
goat has a strong, earthy taste. Available in soft, crumbly and firm textures, in various shapes and sizes.
gruyère a hard-rind Swiss cheese with small holes and a nutty, slightly salty, flavour.

parmesan a sharp-tasting, dry, hard cheese, made from skim or part-skim milk and aged for at least a year.
provolone a mild stretched-curd cheese similar to mozzarella when young, becoming hard, spicy and grainy as it ages. Golden yellow in colour, with a smooth waxy rind.
ricotta a white, soft, sweet, moist, cow-milk cheese with a low-fat content and a slightly grainy texture.

chickpeas also called garbanzos, hummus or channa; an irregularly round, sandy-coloured legume.

chinese barbecued duck traditionally cooked in special ovens, this duck has a sweet-sticky coating made from soy sauce, sherry, five-spice and hoisin sauce. Available from Asian food stores.

chinese cooking wine made from rice, wheat, sugar, salt and alcohol; available from Asian food stores. Mirin or sherry can be substituted.

choy sum also known as pakaukeo or flowering cabbage; a member of the buk choy family. Has long stems, light green leaves and yellow flowers; is eaten stems and all.

ciabatta in Italian, the word means slipper, which is the traditional shape of this popular crisp-crusted white bread.

coriander also known as cilantro or chinese parsley; bright-green-leafed herb with a pungent flavour. Also sold as seeds, whole or ground.

cornflour also known as cornstarch; used as a thickening agent in cooking.

cumin also known as zeera.

curry leaves available fresh and dried; buy fresh leaves at Indian food shops. Remove leaves before serving.

curry pastes
green hottest of the traditional Thai pastes, particularly good in chicken and vegetable curries; also a great addition to stir-fry and noodle dishes.
red probably the most popular curry paste; a hot blend of different flavours that complements the richness of pork, duck and seafood. Also works well in marinades and sauces.

egg some recipes in this book call for raw or barely cooked eggs; exercise caution if there is a salmonella problem in your area.

fennel also known as finocchio or anise; also the name given to dried seeds having a licorice flavour.

fish sauce also called nam pla or nuoc nam; made from pulverised salted fermented fish, most often anchovies. Has a pungent smell and strong taste, so use sparingly.

flat-leaf parsley also known as continental or Italian parsley.

harissa a North African paste made from dried red chillies, garlic, olive oil and caraway seeds. Available ready-made from Middle Eastern food shops.

kaffir lime leaves glossy dark green leaves joined end to end to form a rounded hourglass shape. A strip of fresh lime peel can be substituted for each kaffir lime leaf.

kumara the Polynesian name of an orange-fleshed sweet potato.

galangal the dried root of a plant of the ginger family.

ghee also known as clarified butter; has the milk solids removed. It has a high smoking point so can be heated to a high temperature without burning.

hoisin sauce a thick, sweet and spicy Chinese sauce made from salted fermented soy beans, onions and garlic.

lamington pan 20cm x 30cm slab cake pan, 3cm deep.

lemon grass a tall, lemon-smelling and tasting grass; the white lower part of each stem is used in cooking.

lentils, french green Australian grown and a local cousin to the French import, lentils du puy. They have a sensational nutty, earthy flavour and stand up well to being boiled without becoming muddy.

mince also known as ground meat, as in beef, veal, lamb, pork and chicken.

mushrooms

dried black fungus also known as cloud ear, wood fungus and jelly mushroom. Has a crunchy texture, but little flavour of its own, however, it absorbs the seasonings it is cooked with.

dried porcini also known as cèpes. Has a strong, rich, nutty flavour; must be rehydrated before use.

shiitake when fresh are also known as chinese black, forest or golden oak mushrooms; large and meaty with the earthiness and taste of wild mushrooms. When dried, are also known as donko or dried chinese mushrooms; rehydrate before use.

straw also known as paddy straw or grass mushrooms; seldom available fresh, but easily found canned or dried in Asian grocery stores. They have an intense, earthy flavour.

swiss brown also known as roman or cremini; light to dark brown with full-bodied flavour. Button or cap mushrooms can be substituted.

noodles

rice stick also known as sen lek, ho fun or kway teow; come in thick or thin widths – all should be soaked in hot water until soft.

rice vermicelli similar to bean threads, only they're longer and made with rice flour instead of mung-bean starch.

soba thin, pale-brown noodle originally from Japan; made from buckwheat and varying proportions of wheat flour. Available fresh or dried.

udon available fresh and dried; a broad, white, Japanese wheat noodle.

okra also known as bamia or lady fingers. A green ridged, oblong pod with a furry skin.

pancetta cured pork belly; bacon can be substituted.

paprika ground dried red capsicum (bell pepper); available sweet or hot.

pearl barley the husk is removed, then hulled and polished so that the "pearl" of the original grain remains, much the same as white rice.

polenta also known as cornmeal; a flour-like cereal made of dried corn (maize). Also the name of the dish made from it.

prawns also known as shrimp.

ready-rolled puff pastry packaged sheets of frozen puff pastry.

rocket also known as arugula, rugula and rucola; a peppery green leaf.

sausage

chorizo a sausage of Spanish origin, made of coarsely ground pork and highly seasoned with garlic and chillies.

merguez a spicy sausage of Tunisian origin; made with lamb and identified by its uncooked chilli-red colour.

snow peas also called mange tout (eat all). *Snow pea tendrils* are the growing shoots of the plant.

soy sauce also known as sieu; made from fermented soybeans.

squash, patty pan also known as crookneck or custard marrow pumpkins; round, slightly flat, yellow to pale green in colour with a scalloped edge.

star anise a dried star-shaped pod with an astringent aniseed flavour.

sugar

caster also known as superfine or finely granulated table sugar.

palm also known as nam tan pip, jaggery, jawa or gula melaka; made from the sap of the sugar palm tree. Light brown to black in colour and usually sold in rock-hard cakes; palm sugar can be substituted with brown sugar, if unavailable.

Tabasco brand-name of an extremely fiery sauce made from vinegar, hot red chillies and salt.

tamarind concentrate commercial distillation of tamarind pulp into a condensed, compacted paste. Used straight from the container, with no soaking or straining required; can be diluted with water according to taste.

vietnamese mint not a mint at all, but a pungent and peppery narrow-leafed member of the buckwheat family; also known as cambodian mint, pak pai, laksa leaf, daun kesom and rau ram.

wonton wrappers ready-made wrappers of flour and water. Gow gee and spring roll wrappers can be used as substitutes.

zucchini also known as courgette.

Conversion Chart

MEASURES

One Australian metric measuring cup holds approximately 250ml; one Australian metric tablespoon holds 20ml; one Australian metric teaspoon holds 5ml.

The difference between one country's measuring cups and another's is within a two- or three-teaspoon variance, and will not affect your cooking results. North America, New Zealand and the United Kingdom use a 15ml tablespoon.

All cup and spoon measurements are level. The most accurate way of measuring dry ingredients is to weigh them. When measuring liquids, use a clear glass or plastic jug with the metric markings.

We use large eggs with an average weight of 60g.

DRY MEASURES

METRIC	IMPERIAL
15g	½oz
30g	1oz
60g	2oz
90g	3oz
125g	4oz (¼lb)
155g	5oz
185g	6oz
220g	7oz
250g	8oz (½lb)
280g	9oz
315g	10oz
345g	11oz
375g	12oz (¾lb)
410g	13oz
440g	14oz
470g	15oz
500g	16oz (1lb)
750g	24oz (1½lb)
1kg	32oz (2lb)

LIQUID MEASURES

METRIC	IMPERIAL
30ml	1 fluid oz
60ml	2 fluid oz
100ml	3 fluid oz
125ml	4 fluid oz
150ml	5 fluid oz (¼ pint/1 gill)
190ml	6 fluid oz
250ml	8 fluid oz
300ml	10 fluid oz (½ pint)
500ml	16 fluid oz
600ml	20 fluid oz (1 pint)
1000ml (1 litre)	1¾ pints

LENGTH MEASURES

METRIC	IMPERIAL
3mm	⅛in
6mm	¼in
1cm	½in
2cm	¾in
2.5cm	1in
5cm	2in
6cm	2½in
8cm	3in
10cm	4in
13cm	5in
15cm	6in
18cm	7in
20cm	8in
23cm	9in
25cm	10in
28cm	11in
30cm	12in (1ft)

OVEN TEMPERATURES

These oven temperatures are only a guide for conventional ovens.
For fan-forced ovens, check the manufacturer's manual.

	°C (Celsius)	°F (Fahrenheit)	Gas Mark
Very slow	120	250	½
Slow	150	275-300	1-2
Moderately slow	160	325	3
Moderate	180	350-375	4-5
Moderately hot	200	400	6
Hot	220	425-450	7-8
Very hot	240	475	9

Index

ARE YOU MISSING SOME OF THE WORLD'S FAVOURITE COOKBOOKS?

The Australian Women's Weekly Cookbooks are available from bookshops, cook-shops, supermarkets and other stores all over the world. You can also buy direct from the publisher, using the order form below.

ACP Magazines Ltd Privacy Notice
This book may contain offers, competitions or surveys that require you to provide information about yourself if you choose to enter or take part in any such Reader Offer. If you provide information about yourself to ACP Magazines Ltd, the company will use this information to provide you with the products or services you have requested, and may supply your information to contractors that help ACP to do this. ACP will also use your information to inform you of other ACP publications, products, services and events. ACP will also give your information to organisations that are providing special prizes or offers, and that are clearly associated with the Reader Offer. Unless you tell us not to, we may give your information to other organisations that use it to inform you about other products, services and events or who may give it to other organisations that may use it for this purpose. If you would like to gain access to the information ACP holds about you, please contact ACP's Privacy Officer at ACP Magazines Ltd, 54-58 Park Street, Sydney, NSW 2000, Australia.

☐ **Privacy Notice** Please do not provide information about me to any organisation not associated with this offer.

TITLE	RRP	QTY	TITLE	RRP	QTY
100 Fast Fillets (May 07)	£6.99		Kids' Birthday Cakes	£6.99	
Babies & Toddlers Good Food	£6.99		Kids Cooking	£6.99	
Barbecue Meals In Minutes	£6.99		Kids' Cooking Step-by-Step	£6.99	
Beginners Cooking Class	£6.99		Low-carb, Low-fat	£6.99	
Beginners Simple Meals	£6.99		Low-fat Feasts	£6.99	
Beginners Thai	£6.99		Low-fat Food For Life	£6.99	
Best Food Desserts	£6.99		Low-fat Meals in Minutes	£6.99	
Best Food Fast	£6.99		Main Course Salads	£6.99	
Best Food Mains	£6.99		Mexican	£6.99	
Cafe Classics	£6.99		Middle Eastern Cooking Class	£6.99	
Cakes, Bakes & Desserts	£6.99		Midweek Meals in Minutes	£6.99	
Cakes Biscuits & Slices	£6.99		Moroccan & the Foods of North Africa	£6.99	
Cakes Cooking Class	£6.99		Muffins, Scones & Breads	£6.99	
Caribbean Cooking	£6.99		New Casseroles	£6.99	
Casseroles	£6.99		New Classics	£6.99	
Casseroles & Slow-Cooked Classics	£6.99		New Curries	£6.99	
Cheap Eats	£6.99		New Finger Food	£6.99	
Cheesecakes: baked and chilled	£6.99		New French Food	£6.99	
Chicken	£6.99		New Salads	£6.99	
Chicken Meals in Minutes	£6.99		Party Food and Drink	£6.99	
Chinese Cooking Class	£6.99		Pasta Meals in Minutes	£6.99	
Christmas Cooking	£6.99		Potatoes	£6.99	
Chocolate	£6.99		Salads: Simple, Fast & Fresh	£6.99	
Cocktails	£6.99		Saucery	£6.99	
Cookies	£6.99		Sauces Salsas & Dressings	£6.99	
Cooking for Friends	£6.99		Sensational Stir-Fries	£6.99	
Cupcakes & Fairycakes	£6.99		Slim	£6.99	
Detox	£6.99		Soup	£6.99	
Dinner Lamb	£6.99		Stir-fry	£6.99	
Dinner Seafood	£6.99		Superfoods for Exam Success	£6.99	
Easy Curry	£6.99		Sweet Old-Fashioned Favourites	£6.99	
Easy Spanish-Style	£6.99		Tapas Mezze Antipasto & other bites	£6.99	
Essential Soup	£6.99		Thai Cooking Class	£6.99	
Foods of the Mediterranean	£6.99		Traditional Italian	£6.99	
Foods That Fight Back	£6.99		Vegetarian Meals in Minutes	£6.99	
Fresh Food Fast	£6.99		Vegie Food	£6.99	
Fresh Food for Babies & Toddlers	£6.99		Wicked Sweet Indulgences	£6.99	
Greek Cooking Class	£6.99		Wok, Meals in Minutes	£6.99	
Grills	£6.99				
Healthy Heart Cookbook	£6.99				
Indian Cooking Class	£6.99				
Japanese Cooking Class	£6.99				
Just For One	£6.99		TOTAL COST:	£	

To order: Mail or fax – photocopy or complete the order form above, and send your credit card details or cheque payable to: Australian Consolidated Press (UK), ACP Books, 10 Scirocco Close, Moulton Park Office Village, Northampton NN3 6AP phone (+44) (0)1604 642200 fax (+44) (0)1604 642300 e-mail books@acpuk.com or order online at www.acpuk.com
Non-UK residents: We accept the credit cards listed on the coupon, or cheques, drafts or International Money Orders payable in sterling and drawn on a UK bank. Credit card charges are at the exchange rate current at the time of payment.
Postage and packing UK: Add £1.00 per order plus 50p per book.
Postage and packing overseas: Add £2.00 per order plus £1.00 per book. All pricing current at time of going to press and subject to change/availability.
Offer ends 31.12.2007

Mr/Mrs/Ms _____

Address _____

_____ Postcode _____

Day time phone _____ email* (optional) _____

I enclose my cheque/money order for £ _____

or please charge £ _____

to my: ☐ Access ☐ Mastercard ☐ Visa ___ ☐ Diners Club

PLEASE NOTE: WE DO NOT ACCEPT SWITCH OR ELECTRON CARDS

Card number ☐☐☐☐☐☐☐☐☐☐☐☐☐☐☐☐

Expiry date _____ 3 digit security code *(found on reverse of card)* _____

Cardholder's name_____ Signature _____

* By including your email address, you consent to receipt of any email regarding this magazine, and other emails which inform you of ACP's other publications, products, services and events, and to promote third party goods and services you may be interested in.

If you like this cookbook, you'll love these...

These are just a small selection of titles available in
The Australian Women's Weekly range on sale at selected
newsagents, supermarkets or online at www.acpbooks.com.au

also available in bookstores...

TEST KITCHEN
Food director Pamela Clark
Food editor Karen Hammial
Assistant food editor Sarah Schwikkard
Test Kitchen manager Cathie Lonnie
Senior home economist Elizabeth Macri
Home economists Belinda Farlow, Miranda Farr,
Nicole Jennings, Angela Muscat, Rebecca Squadrito,
Kellie-Marie Thomas, Mary Wills
Nutritional analysis Angela Muscat

ACP BOOKS
Editorial director Susan Tomnay
Creative director & designer Hieu Chi Nguyen
Senior editors Stephanie Kistner, Wendy Bryant

Director of sales Brian Cearnes
Marketing manager Bridget Cody
Production manager Cedric Taylor

Chief executive officer Ian Law
Group publisher Pat Ingram
General manager Christine Whiston
Editorial director (WW) Deborah Thomas

RIGHTS ENQUIRIES
Laura Bamford Director ACP Books
lbamford@acpuk.com

Produced by ACP Books, Sydney.
Printed by Dai Nippon, c/o Samhwa Printing Co Ltd,
237-10 Kuro-Dong, Kuro-Ku, Seoul, Korea
Published by ACP Books, a division of
ACP Magazines Ltd, 54 Park St, Sydney;
GPO Box 4088, Sydney, NSW 2001.
phone (02) 9282 8618 fax (02) 9267 9438.
acpbooks@acpmagazines.com.au
www.acpbooks.com.au

To order books, phone 136 116 (within Australia).
Send recipe enquiries to:
recipeenquiries@acpmagazines.com.au

Australia Distributed by Network Services,
phone +61 2 9282 8777
fax +61 2 9264 3278
networkweb@networkservicescompany.com.au
United Kingdom Distributed by Australian
Consolidated Press (UK),
phone (01604) 642200 fax (01604) 642300
books@acpuk.com
Canada Distributed by Whitecap Books Ltd,
phone (604) 980 9852
fax (604) 980 8197
customerservice@whitecap.ca
www.whitecap.ca
New Zealand Distributed by Netlink
Distribution Company,
phone (9) 366 9966 ask@ndc.co.nz
South Africa Distributed by PSD Promotions,
phone (27 11) 392 6065/7
fax (27 11) 392 6079/80
orders@psdprom.co.za

Clark, Pamela.
The Australian Women's Weekly soup.
Includes index.
ISBN 978 1 86396 576 7
1. Soups. 2. Clark, Pamela
641.813
© ACP Magazines Ltd 2007
ABN 18 053 273 546